CONTENTS

Isaac Newton

by Patrick Moore

ILLUSTRATED BY PATRICIA CULLEN

G. P. PUTNAM'S SONS
NEW YORK

FIRST AMERICAN EDITION 1958

All rights reserved

Library of Congress Catalog
Card Number: 58-7450

MANUFACTURED IN THE UNITED STATES OF AMERICA

VAN REES PRESS • NEW YORK

ISAAC NEWTON

LIVES TO REMEMBER

Chapter 1

A SCIENTIST AT SCHOOL

ALMOST three hundred years ago, in a garden in England, a young man watched an apple fall from a tree. That now-famous apple's fall had strange and far-reaching results—among them the launching of man-made earth satellites in the twentieth century. For the young man was Isaac Newton, and his curiosity about what made the apple fall led to his discovering the law of universal gravitation—the force that keeps our new satellites spinning in their orbits around the earth.

Newton's age, like ours, was one of great upheavals, especially in England. He was born in 1642, during the Civil Wars between Cavaliers and Roundheads in the reign of Charles I; he died in 1727, the same year as George I. Between those dates England underwent great changes: the establishment of the Puritan Commonwealth, the Protectorate of Oliver Cromwell, the Restoration of Charles II, the "Glorious Revolution" that drove Charles's successor James II from the throne, the reigns of William and Mary, Queen Anne and the first George. But none of the political revolutions through which he lived was as earth-shaking as the revolution that he himself brought about in man's knowledge of the universe.

Newton was born on Christmas Day 1642, in the little village of Woolsthorpe, Lincolnshire, about seven miles from the town of Grantham. His father, also named Isaac, had been "lord of the manor," but this did not amount to a great deal. Woolsthorpe is only a tiny hamlet, and the Newton estate was made up of little more than a manor house, a farm and a few cottages. Mr. Newton himself died before his son was born, so Isaac never saw his father.

Mrs. Newton was a gentle but capable woman, and when her husband died she took over the whole management of the farm and the Woolsthorpe estate. At first her baby was weak and sickly. "He could have been put inside a quart pot," his mother is supposed to have said, and for a few days Isaac was so delicate that he was not expected to live. It is all the more remarkable, then, that he should have grown up into a healthy man who lived for eighty-five years.

Things cannot have been easy for Mrs. Newton. The Civil War was raging, and she had nobody to help her run the estate. Moreover, money was none too plentiful, since her husband had been an extravagant man who seems to have spent most of the family fortune. After two years, however, her situation changed very much for the better. The rector of the neighboring parish of North Witham, the Rev. Barnabas Smith, was anxious to find a capable wife, and since he was a very shy man he persuaded one of his parishioners to propose to Mrs. Newton on his behalf. Mrs. Newton accepted, and the rector agreed to repair the Woolsthorpe manor house, at the same time allowing Isaac to keep the income from the estate and promising him an extra fifty pounds a year.

As Mr. Smith could not move away from North Witham, Newton's mother went to live in her new husband's house, leaving Isaac at Woolsthorpe in the care of his grandmother. Fortunately Woolsthorpe and North Witham are only a mile or so apart, so Mrs. Smith could still watch over her delicate son, and for the next few years all was well. Isaac went to the village school, where he learned how to read and write, and he seems to have been perfectly happy. So far he had shown no signs of unusual intelligence, and all we know about his early school life is that he was particularly good at constructing models. He did not make friends easily, and he hated any form of physical cruelty, so in many ways he was quite unlike most of the other boys whom he met.

When he was twelve, Isaac was sent to the King's School in Grantham—so called because it had been founded over a century before by Henry VIII. Here again he showed no great ability, and for his first few terms he remained very near the bottom of his class. Then came an incident which seemed unimportant at the time but which had far-reaching results. A boy who was ahead of Newton in class jeered at him and kicked him. A fight followed, ending only when Newton had beaten his tormentor and rubbed his nose against the wall. This fight, perhaps the only one in which Newton ever took part, made him realize that he would have to work harder if he was to make his way in the world; and he rose steadily in class until he had reached the top of the school.

Isaac learned arithmetic, geometry, history, Latin and Scripture, and by the time he was sixteen he knew as much as (though no more than) most boys of his age. However, he was still interested mainly in his models. Fortunately he boarded in Grantham with an apothecary, Mr. Clark, who was a close friend of his mother's and who helped and encouraged him as much as possible. Isaac's room must have looked like a workshop, with saws, hammers and all sorts of tools strewn around it.

None of Newton's early models have survived, but judging from what we are told they must have been extremely clever. One of them was that of a windmill. Some workmen had been busy building a full-scale windmill near the school, and Newton promptly made

a working model of it, even putting it on top of Mr. Clark's house to catch the wind and keeping a mouse inside it to represent the miller. He also made a water clock, a miniature carriage driven by hand controls somewhat in the manner of a modern invalid chair, a great many paper kites, and a paper lantern which he actually used to light his way as he walked to school in the dark winter mornings.

When Newton was fourteen years old, his stepfather died. Mrs. Smith returned to Woolsthorpe, bringing with her Benjamin, Mary and Hannah, the three children of her second marriage. She had lived quietly and happily at North Witham and did not feel inclined to manage the estate by herself as she had done before; Isaac was growing up, and his mother felt that he was now old enough to be of real help to her, so two years later she took him away from King's School and brought him back home.

It soon became clear that she had made a mistake. Isaac was not in the least interested in managing a farm or an estate, and he had developed a love for pure knowledge which made him quite unfitted for the life of a country gentleman. Although he was devoted to his mother and would have helped her in any way he could, he could not bring himself to concentrate upon such details as the buying and selling of bullocks. He often had to go into the town on farm business, but as soon as he reached Grantham he would make for Mr. Clark's house and spend his time in the attic studying books on chemistry and mathematics, while a farm servant carried out the estate business for him. It was now, perhaps, that he first became really interested in "alchemy," the supposed art of making gold out of less precious metals. Gold making had been a dream of countless men before him, and it proved to be beyond the powers even of Newton, but his study of the problem did at least lead to his gaining a wide knowledge of true chemistry.

He was equally useless when he stayed at home on the farm. He turned his bedroom into a workshop like the one he had made in Mr. Clark's house, and he went on making models, drawing pictures and carrying out scientific experiments. For instance, he made a number of sundials, and some of these can still be seen on the walls of the Woolsthorpe manor house. While he was supposed to be watching the farm laborers, he spent most of his time sitting behind a hedge working out problems in arithmetic and geometry. As a matter of fact he had not yet shown any special interest in mathematics, but he was obviously cut out for the career of a scholar rather than that of a farmer.

Two of the notebooks he kept during this period still survive. One of them, which must have been started while he was still at King's School, contains a number of drawings and paintings as well as details of his models. He was also interested in medicine, and he gives an account of "an excellent plaster for corns" which he made, though we cannot tell whether it was ever used.

Many women in the position of Newton's mother would have made the boy put away all thoughts of science and prepare himself for the time when he would have to take over the whole management of the Woolsthorpe estate. Fortunately Mrs. Smith realized that Isaac was capable of greater things, and accordingly she sent him back to King's School to carry on with his interrupted studies. Then she talked matters over with her brother, the Rev. William Ayscough. Mr. Ayscough was a graduate of Trinity College, part of Cambridge University, and he was wise enough to see that the only course for Isaac was to go to the university.

Even in those days, the twin universities of Oxford and Cambridge were the chief seats of learning in England. Oxford had been founded in the twelfth century, and Cambridge followed not long afterward. Trinity, where Mr. Ayscough had graduated, had been formed during the sixteenth century by the merging of two older colleges. Many famous men have studied there, but when Mr. Ayscough talked to Isaac's mother he had no idea that he was discussing the boy who was to become the most famous of them all. We can only be grateful to him that he decided as he did. Had Isaac Newton been forced to become a farmer, it is possible that his genius would never have developed fully.

The troubles and trials of the Civil War period had died away, at least temporarily. In 1660 King Charles II was recalled from exile to sit upon the throne, and in 1661 Isaac Newton was enrolled as a humble and undistinguished student of Trinity College.

Chapter 2

THE CAMBRIDGE STUDENT

WHEN Newton reached Cambridge, he found that his new companions were very different from the people he had known in Lincolnshire. The Commonwealth was over, and the Puritan rulers had been replaced by the gay, selfish court of Charles II. This gaiety was felt even in the universities, and the students at Trinity College were wild and noisy, so at first Newton felt very ill at ease among them.

He had outgrown his physical weaknesses, and from a delicate boy he had become a healthy young man, but he was still very shy and slow to make friends; nor did he enjoy mixing with rowdy companions. Unluckily he was given a room to share with another undergraduate who was fond of giving parties that went on well after midnight, and we are told that Newton used to wander about the Great Court of the College in the early hours of the morning rather than join in. One night he happened to come across another student who also was taking a late stroll to escape from a similar party given by his roommate. This was the answer to his problem. Newton and the second student decided to exchange roommates, so that they could share a room together well away from the noise.

During his first years as an undergraduate Newton showed normal ability, but little more, and there were few outward signs of the brilliance that he was soon to develop. Some of his notebooks have come down to us, however, and they are of real interest. One of them contains some jottings about the "Copernican theory," and since much of Newton's later work was concerned with astronomy it is worth while pausing for a moment to say something more about old ideas of the universe.

Naturally enough, the earliest men believed the earth to be flat. That this was a mistake was first recognized by the scientists of ancient Greece. Pythagoras, who lived five hundred years before Christ, knew that instead of being flat the earth is shaped like a globe. The later Greeks went even further and found that the sun, moon and stars are tremendously remote, although since they had no telescopes or proper measuring instruments it was not possible to estimate the distances at all accurately.

Despite all their magnificent work, the Greek scientists made one serious error. They believed that the earth lay at rest in the center of the universe, with all the other celestial bodies revolving around it. It is true that Aristarchus of Samos, who died in 250 B.C., suggested that the earth went around the sun; but Aristarchus' ideas were not popular, and after a time they were almost forgotten. The great astronomer Ptolemy wrote a book in which he described the universe as it was believed to be: the earth in the center, with the moon, the sun, the five known planets and the stars revolving at various distances.

Ptolemy died in A.D. 180, and for over a thousand years his system of the universe was thought to be the correct one. It was supported by the Christian Church, which held that it would be irreligious to take the earth away from its proud position of supreme importance. At last, in 1546, a Polish astronomer named Copernicus published a book with the Latin title of *De Revolutionibus Orbium Coelestium* (Concerning the Revolutions of the Heavenly Bodies), in which he showed that instead of the sun going around the earth, the earth and the other planets move around the sun.

Copernicus was well aware that his theory was likely to be attacked by the Church, and he was wise enough not to publish his book until the end of his life. It is said that he was handed the first printed copy only a few hours before he died; and whether this is true or not, we do at least know that he did not live to hear the arguments which raged during the following years.

When we look up at the stars, we can see that they

appear to move across the sky from east to west in the same manner as the sun. The old scientists thought this motion to be real, but Copernicus knew that it is due simply to the spinning of the earth. There is an easy way of showing precisely what is meant by this. If we drive along in a car, the countryside will seem to flash by; but it is the car that is moving, not the houses and trees.

Although Copernicus' theory was bitterly attacked, it had become generally accepted by the time Newton entered Cambridge. There were, however, a great many things still not understood, because although astronomers knew "how" the planets revolved around the sun they did not know "why." It was left to Newton to supply the answer.

The jottings left in these early notebooks show that even as an undergraduate Newton was keenly interested in the mathematics of astronomy, but at first he found that his knowledge was not great enough for him to understand even the easier aspects of it. He therefore bought a book written by the French scientist Descartes, who had died while Newton himself was still a schoolboy at Woolsthorpe.

Descartes' book was not easy to read, since it had purposely been made difficult to follow, and the ordinary student would probably have failed to understand it without help and instruction; but Newton was no ordinary student, and before long he had mastered the whole book. It was about this time, in 1663, that he had another piece of good fortune: he became the pupil of Professor Isaac Barrow.

Newton had already met with kindness and understanding from Mr. Clark, as well as from his mother and his uncle. If it had not been for them he might have been condemned to a country life for which he was totally unfitted, and he might have ended his days as an unsuccessful farmer. Now that he was at Cambridge, he could not have studied under a better teacher than Barrow, who was himself a remarkable man—a brilliant mathematician in his own right, but very different in character from the shy, retiring Lincolnshire youth.

Barrow, son of a linen draper, was thirty-three years old when Newton first began to work under him. Like Newton, he had done little work during his first few years at school and had distinguished himself only by his fondness for fighting. Physically he was very strong, in spite of his small size, and as he won many more fights than he lost he was held in respect by the other boys.

Also like Newton, he at last made up his mind to work really hard. He went to Cambridge and became a Fellow of Trinity College. Barrow was, however, a Royalist, and during the Commonwealth he left England and traveled around Europe and Asia Minor. Although he was now a well-known scholar, he still kept his love of fighting, and on one occasion he showed his courage very plainly. During a sea voyage from Leghorn to Smyrna, his ship was attacked by pirates. Barrow was not frightened; he stayed on deck and fought so bravely that the pirate vessel sheered off.

Barrow returned home soon after the end of the Commonwealth and became professor of Greek at Cambridge. Two years later he was appointed to the professorship of geometry at Gresham College, and in 1663 he was appointed to the Lucasian Chair (or professorship) of mathematics, so called because the money to found the appointment had been provided by the will of a Mr. Lucas. This, then, was the man who now became Newton's teacher and guide.

Barrow must have been a strong-minded man as well as a first-rate scholar. He certainly had great influence over Newton, and from the time when the two men first came into contact Newton's genius developed fast. Six years later, Barrow actually resigned the Lucasian Chair in order to allow Newton to take the position, which is a sure proof of his faith in the powers of his quiet pupil.

Newton applied for a scholarship at Trinity College only a year after he had begun to study under Barrow. Barrow examined him personally, along with forty-four other candidates. Newton passed, but not with much distinction, and it is said that his knowledge of Euclid was found to be rather unsatisfactory. Euclid was a geometrician of ancient Greece whose books still

form the basis of modern textbooks, and since Newton
had mastered Descartes without any help it is surprising to find that he knew less about Euclid. There is a
curious reason for it. Euclid's books are made up chiefly
of geometrical proofs, and Newton had apparently
found the proofs so obvious that he had not bothered
to follow just how Euclid had worked them out. He had
even dismissed the textbook as "trifling." After Barrow's remarks, however, he reread it and realized that
Euclid's work was after all more valuable than he had
at first believed.

This in itself shows how much Newton had progressed. He had the ability to "see" a mathematical
answer instinctively, and he often had to go back over
earlier ground in order to work out just how the answer
could be arrived at. Very few people can do this, even
with easy problems in arithmetic, and certainly nobody
has ever done it more accurately or more often than
Newton did.

It would be wrong to suppose that Newton cut himself off entirely from the normal life of a university
student. His expense books, which are still in existence,
show some entries which might have been made by any
undergraduate. In 1665 there is one entry showing that
he had lost fifteen shillings playing cards, while one
pound is accounted for by "several visits to the tavern."
Probably he had begun to find companions who thought

more as he did, particularly as he was now coming to be known as a young man with exceptional powers.

Now, too, he began his researches into the nature of light, which were later to result in some of his greatest contributions to science. In January 1665 he took the examination for the degree of Bachelor of Arts and passed. Whether he was at the top of the lists is not known, as there are no surviving records, but at any rate he does not appear to have had much difficulty.

In the normal way Newton would probably have taken an appointment at Cambridge, but conditions during 1665 and the following year were far from normal. The terrible disease known as bubonic plague had broken out in England, and before long hundreds of people were dying each day. Seventeen thousand Londoners died during August 1665, and over thirty thousand in September. King Charles and his court left London, but even in the country there was no real safety. The total number of deaths was certainly more than half a million; apart from the Black Death of over three centuries earlier, the plague was the worst epidemic ever to have swept England.

Oxford escaped completely, probably because the drainage and sanitation there were better than in most other cities, but Cambridge did not. Cases of plague appeared in the summer of 1665, and the authorities acted without delay. They closed the university and sent all its members, both teachers and students, back to their homes in different parts of the country. Such an action was obviously wise. Once the plague had gained a real foothold in the comparatively crowded colleges, disaster would certainly have followed, and the decision to disband the university came just in time.

Newton left Cambridge in August 1665, just before the plague reached its worst, and went of course to his home in Woolsthorpe. Here he remained for almost a year, and when we include the vacations we see that between the summer of 1665 and the summer of 1667 he spent more time in Lincolnshire than at the university. To an ordinary man this interruption in career would have done a good deal of harm, but in the case of Newton it was fortunate rather than otherwise. He was able to spend his time peacefully, almost free from financial or other worries, and he managed to do an amazing amount of work. Not only did he develop an entirely new branch of mathematics, but he also continued his researches into the behavior of light; it was at Woolsthorpe, too, that he first began to see the answer to the problem set by the movements of the planets.

The years of the plague were among the most miserable in all English history, but they were probably the greatest in the life of Isaac Newton.

Chapter 3

NEWTON AND THE APPLE

THE story of Isaac Newton and the fall of the apple is very well known. Most people have heard it, and yet it is worth repeating—mainly because it is almost certainly true.

According to the tale, Newton was sitting in his Woolsthorpe garden one afternoon after he had so hurriedly left Cambridge, when he saw an apple fall from a tree branch to the ground. As Newton watched, he began to wonder just why the apple had fallen. There must be some definite force which pulled it toward the ground; but what was this force, and how far did it extend? If the tree had been hundreds of miles high instead of only a few feet, would the apple have fallen just the same? Gradually Newton began to see that the force which pulled on the apple was the same as the force which keeps the moon in its path around the earth. This led him on to the idea of "universal gravitation," according to which every particle of matter attracts every other particle with a force which becomes weaker with increasing distance.

Most famous historical stories of this kind are either false or unproved. We are not at all sure whether King Alfred ever burned any cakes; Canute certainly never sat by the seashore until the waves wet his feet, nor did Galileo drop stones off the top of the Leaning Tower of Pisa to prove that heavy bodies fall at the same rate as lighter ones. But the story of Newton and the apple seems to be basically genuine. Though Newton had been unsuccessful as a farmer, he still kept his interest in the Woolsthorpe estate, and a tall apple tree did grow close to the manor house. The tree decayed and was felled many years ago, but a log of wood said to have been cut from it is still in the possession of the Royal Astronomical Society. Moreover, the story is based on good authority; it was first written down by the French author Voltaire, who said that it had been told to him by Newton's niece.

We can try to follow the way in which Newton reasoned, even though he himself may have worked things out in a different manner. If instead of being twenty feet in altitude the tree had towered to twenty miles, the apple would still have fallen, and it would have dropped to the ground gathering speed as it fell. The same would have been the case with a tree two hundred miles high—assuming that one could exist—since the pull of the earth would be felt even there. Now let us picture a giant tree 238,000 miles high. If an apple could be dropped from it, that apple too would presumably fall to the ground.

The moon, a rocky globe with one-quarter the diameter of the earth, actually does lie at an average distance of just over 238,000 miles—a fact known even in Newton's time. Yet the moon does not fall. Why not?

Newton found the answer: the moon does not drop to the ground for the simple reason that it is moving. It is difficult to give an everyday analogy, but some idea of what is meant can be gathered by taking a spool and whirling it around on the end of a string. The reel will not fall down so long as it continues moving quickly enough to keep the string tight. The earth-moon force acts in much the same way as the string on the spool, so the moon remains at a safe distance.

It is not strictly correct to say that the moon goes around the earth. More accurately, the earth and moon revolve around their common center of gravity, much as the two balls of a dumbbell revolve when the joining bar is twisted. However, the earth is so much more massive than the moon that this center of gravity lies inside the terrestrial globe, and our simple statement is good enough for most purposes. Newton realized this. He also saw that if for any reason the moon's motion were halted, the two bodies would begin to move toward each other until they collided. Fortunately there is no danger of any such disaster; there is no known force capable of stopping a world in its path.

Newton carried his reasoning further. Just as the moon revolves around the earth, so the earth revolves around the sun. Copernicus had demonstrated this, and his work had been improved upon by later astronomers. Here again we can picture the whirling spool, this time

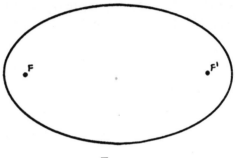

FIG. 1.

with the earth represented by the spool and the sun by the hand holding the string. So long as the earth keeps on moving at its speed of about 66,000 m.p.h. it is in no danger of plunging toward the solar flames, and it keeps on moving simply because there is nothing to stop it.

One of Newton's most important discoveries was finding out the amount by which the pull of a body weakens with increasing distance from it. Before showing how he proved his theory, however, it will be helpful to say something more about what was already known about the movements of the moon and planets.

Copernicus' idea of a sun-centered system was correct, but in other respects he made many mistakes. He supposed, for instance, that the paths (or "orbits") of the planets must be perfect circles, because a circle was a "perfect" form and Copernicus could not bring himself to believe that the heavenly bodies could move in anything but a perfect way.

This led him into serious difficulties. The actual movements of the planets in the sky were known, and they did not fit in with the idea of perfectly circular orbits. Fortunately Copernicus was followed by a Danish astronomer, Tycho Brahe, who made hundreds of accurate observations of the positions of the planets, using instruments that were far better than those available to Copernicus himself; and when Tycho died in 1601 he left all these observations to his assistant, Johann Kepler, who made excellent use of them.

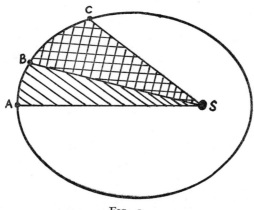

Fig. 2.

Tycho himself never accepted the Copernican theory, and to the day of his death he believed in the old idea of an earth-centered universe, but in this respect at least Kepler was wiser. He saw that circular orbits were impossible, and after many years of patient work he was able to announce the three famous Laws of Planetary Motion that bear his name. They have an important bearing on Newton's work and are not at all hard to understand.

The First Law states that "each planet moves in an ellipse, with the sun in one of the foci." An ellipse is shown in Fig. 1, with the two foci marked F and F'. The distance between F and F' is a measure of the "eccentricity" of the ellipse, and the orbits of the planets are much less eccentric than the figure in the diagram. If F and F' fall at the same point, the figure naturally becomes a circle. In the case of the Earth, F and F' are so close together that the orbit would look circular if drawn on a small scale; but the fact that it is really an ellipse of small eccentricity is most important. The moon's path around the earth is also slightly eccentric.

The Second Law states that "the radius vector of each planet sweeps over equal areas in equal times." The radius vector is an imaginary line joining the center of the sun to the center of the planet, and Fig. 2 will make the law clear. S represents the sun, and A, B and C stand for the planet in various positions in its orbit.

If the planet takes a week to move from A to B, and an equal time to move from B to C, then the triangle SAB must be equal in area to the triangle SBC. This is the case in the diagram, since SAB is the "longer and thinner" of the two. In other words, a planet must move fastest when it is closest to the sun. The same is true for the moon, which moves most quickly when it is nearest to us.

The Third Law gives a definite relationship between a planet's "year," or time of revolution around the sun, and its actual distance from the sun. As we know, the earth's year is 365¼ days, while that of the planet Mars is 687 days. If we know how much longer Mars takes to complete one revolution, we can work out how much farther it must be from the sun. Since the "years" of the various planets can be found out simply by watching how they move, we can work out their distances from the sun compared with that of the earth, and hence draw a complete scale model of the solar system.

All this was known to Newton, who had made a close study of Kepler's books. What he was trying to do now was to find out just why the planets behaved in this manner, and the key to the whole problem lay in the law of "universal gravitation."

Now let us go back to the spool. If the man holding the string suddenly lets go, the spool will fly off in a straight line (dotted in Fig. 3). If we ignore the pull

of the distant sun, the moon too would move in a
straight line, provided the earth did not pull on it.
Newton realized that any moving body will continue
its motion in a straight line unless some outside force
is acting upon it.

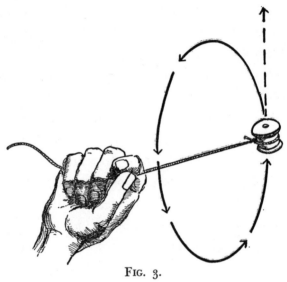

FIG. 3.

The last diagram, Fig. 4, shows the moon's path
around the earth (it is not, of course, to scale). Were
it not for the presence of the earth, we can suppose that
the moon would move from position M to M1 in one
minute. However, the earth is pulling all the time, and
instead of moving in a straight line to M1 the moon is
pulled down to M2; in a way, it has "fallen" from M1
to M2 in one minute, and it goes on "falling" all the
time, though it never drops any closer to the ground.

Newton knew the force of the earth's pull at ground level, since this was the force affecting the apple, and he found the law according to which the force should weaken with increasing distance from the earth. According to his calculations, the moon should "fall" 15 feet per minute, which would of course be the distance between M1 and M2.

Unfortunately this did not agree with observation. The actual distance "fallen" in one minute is not 15 feet, but only 13. In Newton's own words the figures "agreed pretty nearly," but not well enough to satisfy him.

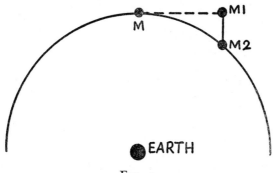

Fig. 4.

For this sort of calculation, a large body such as the earth behaves as though all its mass were concentrated at a single point at the center of the globe. As Newton had to make his observations from the earth's surface, he had of course to know the distance of the surface from the center of the globe—in other words, he had to know the earth's radius (half its diameter) . There is

a famous story that the two-foot error in calculating the
fall of the moon was due to Newton's having used a
wrong value for the radius, and that as soon as a better
measurement became available the error disappeared.
Unlike the tale of the apple, however, this appears to
be nothing more than a story, even though it is still
repeated in many textbooks. Actually one tiny link in
the mathematical argument was still missing, and it was
not until years later that Newton found out what was
wrong.

For the time being he was puzzled, and he laid aside
his work in disappointment. It seemed that his theories
could not be made to fit the observed facts, and he
turned his main attention to other matters.

He had already developed a completely fresh branch
of mathematics, which he called the "Method of Fluxions" but which is known to us as calculus, and he was
busy making experiments on the nature and behavior
of light, as well as continuing his chemical researches,
so he had plenty to do. However, he was not inclined
to publish any of his work, least of all that which was
concerned with the troublesome law of gravitation.

Clearly Newton had not outgrown his boyish shyness
and sensitivity, and in fact he never really did so. He
hated criticism of any kind, and this must have been
one of the reasons why he was so reluctant to make his
work known to other scientists. During the plague years
he was quite content to work on his own without con-

sulting others, and this was also the case after he went back to Cambridge.

We can form a good picture of Newton as he was during those quiet days at Woolsthorpe. He was short, slight and brown-eyed; his jaw was square, his mouth firm and determined, his hair already beginning to turn white. He was not good-looking, partly because of his noticeably long nose, but his face showed an iron strength of will. In manner he is said to have been rather serious, though he grew more jovial in his old age. He realized that he was at the height of his powers, and he himself said that during the two years at Woolsthorpe he "minded mathematics and philosophy more than at any time since."

But he could not stay at home forever. The plague, which had caused such misery in London and other cities, was dying down, and before long the worst of the danger was over. In 1666, therefore, Newton returned to Cambridge to pick up the threads of his life at the university.

Chapter 4

NEWTON'S SEARCH FOR GOLD

WE ARE USED to regarding Isaac Newton as a genius, and there is in fact no doubt that his was one of the finest brains in history. If he had done no more than discover the law of universal gravitation, he would have been worthy to rank with the greatest scientists of his age, but when we add his work on light, his mathematical researches and the rest of his various activities we can appreciate his true brilliance.

On the other hand, it would be a serious mistake to think of Newton as being always right. There were times when he made errors (some of which he admitted later) and now and then he overlooked points which he might well have been expected to see. He considered, for instance, that it would never be possible to make a really good refracting telescope, when actually there was a perfectly simple solution to this particular problem if he had only realized it. But as well as this, there was another side to Newton's character. He was not solely a practical, hard-headed scientist; he was also what is known as a "mystic."

It is not easy to explain precisely what is meant by this term, and perhaps the best way to do so is to say that a mystic is one who seeks to discover hidden truths which lie outside the range of normal experience. All "magic" comes under such a heading. In Newton's time there were two so-called sciences, astrology and alchemy, which were accepted on equal terms with astronomy and physics but which were based on such "magic" and superstition.

Astrology may be defined as "the superstition of the stars." According to it, each heavenly body has an effect upon the life and character of every human being. The most important bodies astrologically are the sun, moon and planets, and it is claimed that their positions in the sky have a powerful and lasting influence upon the destiny of a newborn child. By working out these positions and charting them, an astrologer will claim that he can see into the future.

It is hardly necessary to emphasize that astrology is utter nonsense. The planets are far closer than the fixed stars, and when an astrologer talks about Mars or Jupiter being "in" a constellation—Taurus the Bull, for instance —he is describing nothing more significant than an effect of perspective. All he means is that Mars happens to be seen against a background of stars thought by the ancients to be arranged in a pattern which looked like a bull. Really, the pattern of the stars in Taurus is nothing like a bull or anything else. In any case, we might as well say that a lamppost seen in front of a distant forest is "in" the forest!

All the ancient astronomers were also astrologers. Tycho Brahe was particularly enthusiastic, and even the clear-sighted Kepler earned money by drawing up mystical charts. But as true knowledge grew, astrology naturally faded away, until by Newton's time it had become obvious that no planet or star can have the slightest effect upon the destiny of a man. On the other hand, the second great mystical "science," alchemy, was slower to die. It lasted until well into the following century, and Newton himself was a keen alchemist.

Gold has always been regarded as a very precious substance, partly because of its rarity and partly because of its beauty. Until the present century it was the metal used for coins of high value, and it is still the standard of value for much of the world's currency. Anyone who can obtain a great deal of gold will be rich. Gold can of course be mined, which is the actual way in which it is made available, but it cannot be made from other substances.

There are very good reasons for this, but these reasons were not known until long after the death of Newton, so it was still believed that there might be a way of making gold from less valuable materials such as silver and lead. This gold making was one of the aims of the alchemists. They carried out vast numbers of experiments and spent many years in trying to do what we now know to be impossible. Fortunately their work was not wasted, since although they failed to make gold they did discover much about true chemistry. Gradually, the alchemists of old turned into the chemists of modern times.

It would be wrong to suppose that the making of gold was the only aim of the alchemists. Nor would it be fair to say that they were chiefly interested in making themselves rich. They were searching for hidden truths, and they also hoped to find the key to eternal life and eternal youth; they believed that by "chemical" methods they could unravel all the secrets of the universe.

Newton was no exception. All through his younger days, and all through the period when he was doing his greatest mathematical work, he was busy making alchemical experiments in his laboratory. An assistant who worked for him wrote that Newton used to "employ about six weeks in his laboratory" at a time, "the fire scarcely going out either night or day; he sitting up one night and I another, until he had finished his chemical experiments. . . . What his aim might be I was not able to penetrate into, but his pains, his diligence at these set times made me think he aimed at something beyond the reach of human art and industry."

He must have thought that he had come to the verge

of discovering the secret of life itself, and it was not unreasonable of him to think so. At the time when his assistant wrote the lines quoted above, Newton had already made some discoveries which had altered all the old ideas about science; if he could succeed in practical science, why could he not succeed just as brilliantly in mysticism—particularly as he did not realize that there was any essential difference between the two? Newton never gave up his interest in alchemy, though he did put it aside in later years. Even his genius was not unlimited.

It is not hard to show why the alchemists were doomed to failure from the start. Nowadays it is known that all matter in the universe, whether on the earth or in a remote star system, is made up out of a comparatively small number of fundamental substances or "elements." Water is not an element; the smallest possible particle of water can be broken down into still smaller particles of oxygen and hydrogen. The famous chemical formula H_2O means that one "molecule" of water can be split up into two "atoms" of hydrogen and one of oxygen. On the other hand, it is not possible to break down hydrogen or oxygen any further, since both are elements.

There are ninety-two naturally occurring elements, and all matter is built up from them. It is possible to make elements combine to form compounds, and there is no difficulty in making hydrogen and oxygen unite once more to make ordinary water, but the elements

themselves cannot be manufactured from other substances.

Newton seems to have had some vague ideas about
atoms, but he had no real idea of how matter is built up.
Had he realized that gold is itself an element and cannot be made, he would have been almost two centuries
ahead of his time; but he never did, and to the end of
his life he continued to believe that some alchemist
would one day hit upon the great secret.

In another way, too, this mystical side to his character
showed itself. He spent many hours studying old writ-
ings and old manuscripts in an effort to find hidden
meanings in them, and he left a mass of notes and records which have never been properly studied. Nor does
it seem likely that anyone will take the trouble to do
so, since their very nature makes it clear that they are
completely "magical" and have no scientific value.

In 1942, three centuries after Newton's birth, it was
planned to hold a scientific conference in London to
mark the occasion. It had to be postponed because of
the war, but in 1946 it was held as originally arranged,
and scientists from all over the world came to honor
Newton's memory. One of the papers was written by
Lord Keynes, and it described Newton as a man "with
one foot in the Middle Ages and the other foot tread-
ing a path for modern science." This sums him up
exactly; he saw more clearly into nature than anyone

before him, yet he was still unable to break free from the strange ideas of his predecessors.

Apart from mysticism, about which he was quite frank, there was one branch of study which singled Newton out from his companions, and which he did his best to keep to himself. This concerned religion.

We have to admit that the Church has never been quick to accept new scientific ideas. When Copernicus first showed that the earth revolves around the sun, he was wise enough to delay publishing his theory until he had reached the end of his life—since he feared that he would be attacked by the Christian authorities. Giordano Bruno, a great man and a farsighted scientist, was burned at the stake in 1600; even Galileo was arrested by the Inquisition and threatened with torture unless he abandoned the absurd notion that the earth might revolve around the sun.

Newton began his work after the Church had had to accept the Copernican theory, so he was in no danger of being tortured or burned alive. On the other hand, in those days a man's religion was not purely his own business, as is the case today. Not long after the publication of Newton's greatest book, the *Principia,* King James II of England was driven from his throne because he tried to force Roman Catholicism upon his subjects. Any well-known man who held religious views different from that of the official Church was liable to find himself in trouble.

Newton was a sincere Christian, but he could not think in precisely the same way as most of his companions; he was what is now known as a Unitarian. It would have been an advantage for him to take holy orders and become a clergyman, but he could not bring himself to do so, which is an extra proof of his sincerity.

Newton decided to keep his religious views a secret. He left a large wooden chest full of notes, many of which were not published until the present century. It is said that not long after his death the chest was opened by a Church of England bishop, Horsley, who read one or two of the notes and then slammed the lid shut in horror.

Evidently Newton was careful to guard his tongue, and so far as his fellow students were concerned there was nothing strange about him apart from his unusual brilliance. He returned to Cambridge in 1666, after the plague had begun to die away, and in the following year he was elected to a fellowship (a kind of scholarship for graduate students) of Trinity College.

Chapter 5

THE REFLECTING TELESCOPE

NEWTON had left Cambridge before the plague as a young man who had yet to make his mark in the scientific world. Of all his companions, probably only Barrow knew of his true ability. By the time the university reassembled, Newton had already hit upon some remarkable truths: the calculus, the law of gravitation, and some equally important studies about light. Unfortunately Newton was always slow to publish anything, and for the time being he remained silent.

After his election to a fellowship of Trinity College he took the degree of Master of Arts. All this time he was busy working on his own, both at scientific and at mystical matters, but in 1669 came a turning point in his career. Barrow resigned from the Lucasian Chair of mathematics and made it possible for Newton to take his place.

Barrow wanted to spend his future years in studies

other than scientific ones, but he was in any case glad to hand over his professorship to a young man of Newton's genius. Though Barrow was one of the best mathematicians living at the time, his greatest contribution to learning proved to be the opportunity which he gave to Newton.

Things were easier for Newton after his appointment, since the Lucasian Chair meant that he had more money. For the first time, too, he started to give lectures —not because he wanted to, but because lecturing was one of the duties of the Lucasian professor. The subject he chose was optics, the study of light, and much of what he said was completely new to science.

The lectures themselves were not well attended by students, and there were occasions when nobody at all came to listen, but Newton was not at all concerned. He was always happier working by himself than when teaching others. Before long, however, reports of his lectures reached the Royal Society of London for Improving Natural Knowledge, which was (and is) the leading scientific society of Great Britain, and Newton was invited to send communications to it. In December 1671 Dr. Ward, Bishop of Salisbury, proposed Newton for membership in the Society, and in January of the following year he was duly elected.

The meeting of the Society at which Newton was actually admitted as a Fellow was held on January 11, and at the same meeting a paper was read describing his

newly invented "reflecting telescope." Shortly afterward Newton sent to Henry Oldenburg, the secretary
of the Society, a longer and more detailed paper about
light, which was read on February 6. These papers
brought Newton to the notice of scientific men all over
the world and represent his first published work of
major importance—since as yet he had said little about
calculus and nothing at all about the law of gravitation.

All through his quiet period at Woolsthorpe during
the plague years, Newton had spent a great deal of time
studying the behavior of light. The great discovery
which put him onto the right track was that "white"
light is really a mixture of all the colors of the rainbow
—red, orange, yellow, green, blue, indigo and violet.
He proved this by taking a beam of "white" light and
splitting it up by means of a triangular piece of glass
known as a prism; the diagram in Fig. 5 shows the
principle of the actual experiment which he made.

He allowed sunlight to enter a darkened room
through an opening in a shutter. The beam then passed
through the prism, and from the prism onto a screen.
Yet the appearance on the screen was not simply a white
spot, as might have been expected. The spot was about
five times as long as it was broad, with red at one end,
violet at the other and the remaining colors in between.
This effect is known to us as a "spectrum," but such a
thing was quite unknown before Newton's work at
Woolsthorpe.

It did not take him long to find out the reason for this spreading-out of the beam. When the white light passed into the prism, it was broken up, and the different parts were bent or "refracted" unequally. The violet part was the most bent, and so it appeared at the far end of the spectrum on the screen. Indigo light was bent less, blue less still, and so on, red light being bent least of all.

Newton did not stop there. His next experiment was to make a hole in the screen so that only one part of the

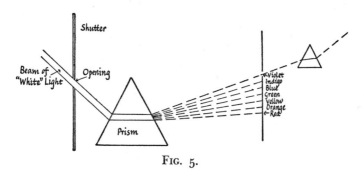

FIG. 5.

spectrum could pass through. When he passed through only the violet light, as in the diagram, it was further bent by a second prism, but this time it was not split up into another spectrum; violet light, unlike white, is not a blend of different colors. When the red beam only was allowed to pass into the second prism it, too, was bent, but less than the violet. By measuring the bending of the different colors, Newton was able to prove his theory beyond any shadow of doubt.

This led him on to consider the telescope, that all-important tool of the astronomer, and it was in this connection that he made one of his few real mistakes.

FIG. 6.

Telescopes of the early seventeenth century were refractors and used lenses to collect their light. The principle of a refractor is shown in Fig. 6. The light from the star, or whatever object is to be studied, is collected by a lens known as an object glass (OG), shaped so as to bunch all the rays together at one point, the focus (F). The distance between OG and F is known as the focal length. The image at F is then magnified by a second lens called an eyepiece (EP). Telescopes of this kind had been invented over thirty years before Newton's birth; they had first been turned to the heavens by Galileo, who had played a great part in laying the foundations of experimental science.

The first refractors were not satisfactory, however, since a bright object such as a star was always surrounded by false color. It had been supposed that this trouble was due to the object glass not being shaped properly, and in order to correct it the telescope makers of the time constructed instruments of enormous focal length. Sometimes the object glass had to be slung up in the air, while the observer peered through the eyepiece many feet away from the main lens. Aerial telescopes of this kind were extremely difficult to use, and even then they did not wholly get rid of the false-color trouble.

As soon as Newton made his experiments with the prism, he saw what was wrong. The trouble was due not to the object glass, but to the nature of light itself. A beam of light entering the object glass would be split up in the same way as in the prism, and since the red light would be bent less than the violet it would be brought to focus in a different place. False color was bound to result. This is shown in Fig. 7, in which the difference in bending has been deliberately drawn as more marked than is really the case.

So far, so good. Newton had shown that it is not possible to make a good refracting telescope so long as the object glass is made up of a single lens. There is, however, a solution to the problem. In all modern refractors the object glass is not just a single lens but is made up of two or more lenses made of different kinds of glass, so that the errors do not add up. The false-color trouble

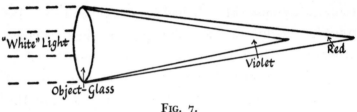

Fig. 7.

can never be corrected completely, but it can be greatly reduced. Oddly enough the idea of using a compound object glass did not occur to Newton, and he decided that to try to build a large and color-free refractor would be a sheer waste of time.

For some time he put the telescope problem aside, but he did not neglect optics in general. For instance, he produced a grayish pigment made by combining artists' colors in definite proportions. This was put on the floor together with a piece of white paper, and when a beam of sunlight was allowed to fall onto the two it was seen that the pigment actually looked the "whiter." He also examined the colors produced by films of transparent material, such as soap bubbles, and worked out a method of measuring the thicknesses of the films responsible.

After his return to Cambridge, Newton began to consider the problem of making an astronomical telescope which would collect light without causing false color, and he decided to abandon lenses completely. He turned instead to mirrors and constructed a "reflecting" telescope which did not use an object glass at all. The basic idea was not entirely new, as it had been put forward some years before by a Scottish scientist named Gregory. However, Gregory "had no practical skill," as he was the first to admit, and to Newton goes the honor of making the first reflector. Moreover, the arrangement which he used was not precisely the same as Gregory's.

In Newton's reflector, the light from the star passes straight down an open tube until it hits a curved mirror at the bottom, as is shown in Fig. 8. This mirror bunches the light rays together and directs them onto a smaller mirror or "flat," placed at an angle. This in turn produces the image of the star at the focal point F, where it passes into the eyepiece lens in the usual way.

The advantage here is that while the light has to pass *through* the object glass of a refractor, it does not have to pass through the mirror of an instrument built on Newton's pattern. The light is merely reflected, and all the rays, from red to violet, are reflected equally. Consequently there is no fear of any false color being caused.

Fig. 8.

Newton's first reflector was made at about the time of his appointment to the Lucasian Chair, but (as usual) he made no announcement at that moment. It was not until his paper was read to the Royal Society that the discovery became known, and it caused a tremendous amount of interest. He soon made a second and rather better reflector, which he sent to the Royal Society. This instrument still exists, and it is one of the Society's most treasured possessions. It has a mirror only one inch in diameter, but it was the forerunner of all the great reflectors made in later years—including the 200-inch giant now standing on Mount Palomar, California. A drawing of Newton's telescope is given in Fig. 9.

It must be remembered that Newton built the whole instrument himself: mirror, tube, mounting, eyepiece and all. The mirror was made of a mixture of copper and tin, which gives the surface an almost silvery shine; in a letter to Oldenburg, Newton gave some details of the method used: "I first melted the copper alone, then put in some arsenic, which being melted I stirred them a little together, bewaring, in the meantime, that I draw not in breath near the pernicious fumes. After that I put in the tin, and again, so soon as that was melted, which was very suddenly, I stirred them well together, and immediately poured them off." The final instrument gave a magnification of about thirty-eight times.

The reflector was examined by some of England's most learned men, such as the inventor Robert Hooke and the famous architect Sir Christopher Wren. It was also examined by King Charles II, who took a great interest in it. History books in general are rather unkind to Charles; it is true that he was a shallow, selfish man who put himself before his country, but he had many good points, and whether his motives were sound or not he certainly did much for science. It was due to Charles that Greenwich Observatory was founded; the king was always friendly to the Royal Society, to which he himself had given its first charter, and to Newton personally.

Not all the comments upon Newton's optical work were favorable. It is true that little criticism could be leveled at the telescope itself, which was obviously a brilliant invention, but some of Newton's theories about light were promptly attacked. The chief critic was Robert Hooke, who was later to play an important part in Newton's life. Unfortunately Newton was quick to take offense and he took a great deal of trouble to point out the mistakes of his opponents, which led him into a series of bitter disputes.

FIG. 9.

Newton was no longer an obscure university professor. He had become famous throughout the world, but
this made no difference to his shyness, his hatred of
criticism, and his reluctance to publish his results.
However, before turning to the next stage of his career,
which ended in the publication of his immortal book
the *Principia,* we must pay some attention to the other
men with whom his life was to be linked.

Chapter 6

NEWTON'S FRIENDS AND ENEMIES

NEWTON's shy, sensitive character did not lead him to make many close friends. On the other hand, he was always happy in his family life. He was devoted to his mother, and her death soon after the publication of the *Principia* was a great grief to him; he was generous to his relatives, and later his niece, Catherine Barton, kept house for him for many years.

He never married. When he entered Cambridge he was engaged to Miss Storey, the stepdaughter of that Mr. Clark with whom he had stayed in Grantham and who had encouraged him in his model making, but at some point during his career as an undergraduate the engagement was broken off. There was evidently no quarrel, or even suspicion of a quarrel, and Newton and Miss Storey remained on the best of terms throughout their lives. Both seemed to have realized that marriage would have been a mistake, and that Newton could never have put his private life before his science.

Most of those with whom Newton came into contact must have been acquaintances rather than friends, since it has been said (with a good deal of truth) that he was unable to work with anybody upon equal terms. Edmond Halley must be called a true friend; but Halley was much younger than Newton, treated him with respect, and realized that Newton's gifts were greater than his own.

A man who played a considerable part in Newton's career was the famous Sir Christopher Wren. Wren is best remembered as the architect who rebuilt St. Paul's Cathedral after the Fire of London in 1666; but he also designed many buildings elsewhere, including the library of Trinity College, and he was responsible for the plan of the original observatory at Greenwich, which still stands in its old position, although the instruments and staff have now left the smoky suburb in favor of the clearer air of Sussex.

It comes as a surprise to most people to learn that Wren did not begin his career as an architect at all, but as an astronomer. Eleven years older than Newton, he took his degrees at Oxford. In 1657 he became professor of astronomy at Gresham College, and in 1660, before Newton reached Cambridge, Wren was appointed Savilian Professor of Astronomy at Oxford. He was a first-class mathematician, and had he kept to science he would certainly have made a great reputation for himself, but after a while his other interests drew him away from Oxford. He entered Parliament and did little more serious scientific study, though he kept closely in touch with the leading scientists and also engaged actively in the business of the Royal Society. Wren seems to have been a pleasant, likable man, and he always remained on excellent terms with Newton.

Robert Hooke, also a prominent member of the Royal Society, was of a very different type. He was a brilliant scientist and inventor, and it is a great pity that he is now remembered mainly because of his bitter quarrels with Newton and others.

Hooke, seven years older than Newton, took his Master of Arts degree at Oxford while Newton was still an undergraduate at Cambridge. Unfortunately he was physically weak, and it is said of him that "his figure was crooked, his limbs shrunken; his hair hung in dishevelled locks over his haggard countenance. His temper was irritable, his habits solitary." It is clear that Hooke's was far from an attractive personality, and he was violently jealous and suspicious, so he made enemies more easily than friends.

Hooke's activities spread into all scientific fields. He invented the "universal joint" known to every mechanic; he made some meteorological instruments, such as a hygrometer (a device for measuring the wetness of the air) and a registering rain gauge; he also carried out important experiments concerning sound.

Another idea of his was to fit a telescope with a clock. The earth's rotation causes all the heavenly bodies to drift slowly and steadily across the sky, and a star will soon move out of the field of view of a motionless telescope. Hooke's remedy was to drive the telescope gradually around by means of a clock, at such a rate that it followed the star's motion and kept it in the field of visibility. All large telescopes of today are driven in such a fashion. Hooke also developed the study of past earth history by investigating fossils, the remains of long-dead plants and creatures, much in the way that Leonardo da Vinci had done; he was, moreover, an excellent architect and watchmaker, and it was he who first suggested regulating a watch movement by means of a balance spring. Even more important were his improvements to the microscope.

All this work shows that Hooke was a remarkably clever man. Yet he studied so many things that he never followed any particular branch through to the end, as Newton did, and he had the habit of claiming as his own discoveries which had actually been made by others. Frequently there was a germ of truth in these claims. The balance spring of the watch, for instance, was certainly first thought out by him, but the Dutch scientist Christiaan Huygens developed it independently and produced a far better version, which led to a furious argument when Hooke accused Huygens point-blank of copying his invention.

This is not to imply that Hooke was dishonest. He was perfectly well-meaning, but he was unable to argue without becoming unpleasant, and Newton was particularly sensitive to such an attitude. Nothing could have prevented bad feeling between two such men, though each respected the ability of the other.

The first clash came when Newton presented his reflecting telescope to the Royal Society. Hooke made some criticisms of it and stated that he himself had made a reflector as long ago as 1664. Actually there is no proof of this claim, but it would be hasty to say that it is entirely false; Hooke may have produced a small telescope (he must have heard of the original suggestion made by Gregory), though since he did not share Newton's dislike of publicity one wonders why he made no announcement.

However, the real storm broke when Hooke attacked the theories of light put forward by Newton in his second paper to the Royal Society. He admitted the effectiveness of the reflector itself, but he more or less advised Newton to content himself with practical work and leave the theories to men more qualified to understand them.

Newton naturally made a full reply. He began by saying that "Mr. Hooke thinks himself concerned to reprehend me. . . . But he knows well it is not for one man to prescribe rules to the studies of another, especially with not understanding the grounds on which he proceeds." Hooke was furious, and the quarrel was never really cleared up. It did die down for a time, but began again some years later over a totally different matter.

Although Newton was quick to answer any attacks made on him, he hated argument of any kind. Consequently he refused to publish much of his optical work as long as Hooke lived, since he knew that fresh disputes were bound to arise. Hooke died in 1703, and in the following year Newton at last published his most important studies concerning light in the form of a book, *Opticks*.

Newton and Hooke were both Fellows of the Royal Society, and had the secretary there been a man friendly to both of them it might have been possible to patch things up. Unhappily the secretary of the Royal Society at the time when Newton began to publish his papers was Henry Oldenburg, who hated Hooke and stirred up as much trouble as he could.

The exact cause of Oldenburg's dispute with Hooke is of no real interest, and it is not even certain who was to blame, though the trouble probably began with some of Hooke's usual rudeness. At any rate, Oldenburg did his best to annoy Hooke as much as possible. There were periods when Hooke and Newton were on fairly good terms, particularly between 1673 and 1679, but Oldenburg usually managed to upset matters once more. Once, for instance, Newton sent Oldenburg a polite message to pass on to Hooke, and there are grounds for supposing that Oldenburg purposely kept it back.

On the other hand Oldenburg was perfectly friendly toward Newton and even went out of his way to help him. In March 1673 Newton asked to be allowed to resign from the Royal Society, mainly because each Fellow was bound to make a weekly payment and Newton had little money to spare. He was not in holy orders, and in the normal way his fellowship of Trinity College was due to end in 1675. Actually Charles II smoothed out these difficulties by a special order which allowed Newton to stay as Lucasian Professor without entering the Church, but by that time Oldenburg had already persuaded the council of the Royal Society to excuse Newton from the weekly payments. When Oldenburg died, in 1677, Hooke succeeded him as secretary.

Hooke was not the only man to criticize Newton's theories of light. Huygens, probably the best telescopic astronomer of the day, also did so, and others were Linus and Lucas of Liége. Scientific arguments should be carried on without personal bad feeling, but Newton was obviously annoyed, particularly with Lucas.

Another leading figure who came into conflict with Newton was John Flamsteed, the first Astronomer Royal. Flamsteed was four years younger than Newton, and he, too, went to Cambridge, taking his Master of Arts degree in 1674. By then he was already becoming known as a skillful astronomer, and he had met Newton, with whom he was at first on friendly terms.

England has always been a seafaring nation, and in those days the only way to navigate a ship accurately was by making observations of the moon and stars. Unfortunately the best star catalogue available, Tycho Brahe's, was still not good enough to meet the needs of the seamen, and Charles II ordered that the stars should be "measured and examined anew." Greenwich Observatory was founded, and the first building, designed by Wren, was begun in 1675—the money being raised by the sale of "old and decayed gunpowder." Flamsteed was appointed Astronomer Royal, and in due course he did in fact produce a star catalogue that was far better than Tycho's.

Flamsteed was a touchy, irritable man who suffered from ill-health, and he too was slow to publish his results, not because he objected to criticism but because he disliked being hurried. When Newton wanted some particular information and Flamsteed was reluctant to provide it, a bitter quarrel began which lasted until Flamsteed's death in 1719. Flamsteed was mainly to blame, but Newton himself was far from faultless, and the letters and documents which passed between them were hardly creditable to either party.

Newton's relations with the other great astronomer of the period, Edmond Halley, were much more friendly. Halley must have been a difficult man to quarrel with.

He had none of Newton's sensitiveness or Hooke's irritability, and he did his best to stay on good terms with everyone, though he did not find this possible in the case of Flamsteed.

Born in 1656, Halley at an early age showed himself to be a gifted mathematician. He turned his attention to astronomy, and when only twenty years old, before he had graduated from Oxford, he took his telescope and his measuring instruments to the lonely island of St. Helena to study the southern stars. Unluckily for European observers, some of the most interesting objects in the sky never rise above the horizon in northern latitudes, and until Halley began his work the objects in the far south had never been properly studied. He stayed on St. Helena for a year and managed to do a great deal of valuable work, even though the weather was often bad. When he returned he was given a Master of Arts degree from Oxford, and in 1678 he was elected to the Royal Society.

Halley was never idle. He made other journeys; for instance, he went to Danzig on the Baltic coast to meet the famous observer Hevelius, and he spent some time in Paris as the guest of the director of the Paris Observatory, Cassini. But though Halley is best remembered for his connection with the famous comet now named after him, his greatest work for science was not actually his own. It was Halley who drew Newton's attention back to the law of gravitation, and persuaded him to write the magnificent book *Principia*.

When Flamsteed died, Halley succeeded him as Astronomer Royal at Greenwich, and he held the position until his death in 1742. Halley thus outlived Newton by fifteen years and was the last survivor of the group of brilliant men who argued so forcefully during the days of Charles II.

Perhaps Halley's greatest gift was his readiness to see the strong points of others. He was a good mathematician, but he was by no means the equal of Newton, and when he came across a problem which he could not solve he did not hesitate to take it to Newton and ask for help. One can hardly picture Hooke, Flamsteed or even Newton himself doing as much.

The last of the scientists who influenced Newton's career was one whom he seems never to have met: Gottfried Wilhelm Leibnitz, who was born at Leipzig in 1646. Leibnitz was a brilliant boy who taught himself Latin and could read both it and Greek by the time he was twelve. When he turned his attention to mathematics he revealed a skill almost as great as Newton's, and he developed calculus independently in a form distinctly better than that of Newton.

Leibnitz visited London in 1673 and met Oldenburg, but there is no record of his having seen Newton personally. The two did write to one another in a friendly manner later on, but finally there was a dispute as to who had been the first to discover calculus, and a tedious and bitter battle of words dragged on until Leibnitz died.

Newton's personal friends, as distinct from his scientific acquaintances, do not play much part in the story of his work. There is, however, one important exception: Charles Montague, later Earl of Halifax and Chancellor of the Exchequer. Montague remained loyal even when Newton fell ill and wrote him some strange and wild letters. It was due to his influence that Newton was afterward appointed Warden of the Royal Mint.

In dealing with Newton, one must not neglect these friends and opponents whose careers are associated with his. They are of very different types: the weakly, irritable Hooke, the touchy and sensitive Flamsteed, the courageous Barrow, the good-humored Halley and Montague—each of these men played a part in his life. It has been necessary to say something about each, as otherwise it would not have been possible to build up a complete picture of Newton himself.

At the time when he first became a Fellow of the Royal Society, then, Newton had blossomed forth into one of Europe's leading scientists. His greatest triumph, culminating in the immortal *Principia,* was not to come for another thirteen years.

Chapter 7

NEWTON'S GREATEST WORK

NEWTON's first papers to the Royal Society were concerned almost entirely with light. During his stay at Woolsthorpe, while the plague raged in London, he had of course worked on gravitational problems and on his new branch of mathematics, but all this remained unpublished and unknown, except for one paper which he seems to have shown to Barrow.

Whether Newton would have published his work on gravitation had it not been for the troublesome two-foot error in calculating the "fall" of the moon is uncertain. He might have done so before his first clashes with Hooke, but afterward he knew that Hooke and others were only too ready to criticize him. Rather than be drawn into an argument, he preferred to keep silent.

In 1675, however, he did mention one important discovery in a letter to Nicolas Mercator, the map maker (many modern charts are drawn on Mercator's projection). This concerned the tilting or "libration" of the moon.

The moon revolves around the earth once a month, and it also spins on its own axis once a month, so it keeps the same face turned permanently toward us. With our telescopes, we can study only part of the moon; there is another part which is always hidden from us, and which we are unable to examine. This sounds somewhat confusing, but a simple experiment will show what is meant.

Put a chair in the middle of the room and let it represent the earth, with your head representing the moon. Your face therefore represents the visible part of the moon, and the back of your head the moon's hidden part.

First walk around the chair in a circle, keeping your eyes fixed upon some background object such as the mantelpiece or a window. By the time you have walked halfway around, you will find that anyone sitting on the chair will be looking at the back of your head. Similarly, if the moon did not spin on its axis it would show us all of its surface at various times.

Now walk around the chair, turning so as to keep your eyes toward it. By the time you have completed one full circuit, you will have turned once "on your axis." This is how the moon behaves, and it is most annoying to the astronomer who wants to study all the lunar surface instead of only part of it.

Yet the moon does seem to tip very slowly to and fro, so it is possible to see for some distance around alternate edges. For a day or two the eastern edge will be tilted toward us; then it will be seen that there is a slight tipping the other way, until after a while the western edge will be best placed. At various times we can examine a total of four sevenths of the lunar surface, while the other three sevenths remains permanently out of view.

These tiltings of "librations" had been known ever since Galileo had turned his original telescope to the skies, but their cause remained unknown. Newton provided the answer. Like the planets, the moon revolves in an orbit that is not perfectly circular, so its distance from the earth varies regularly from 226,000 miles at minimum to 252,000 at maximum. Kepler's second law shows that it must move fastest when at its closest to us. On the other hand, the axial spin is steady and unvarying, so the axial spin and the moon's position in its orbit fall "out of step" at various times every month. This is why the moon seems to us to tilt slightly instead of showing us only an exact half of its surface. (More accurately, it is one of the reasons. There is also a north-south libration due to a rather different cause.)

The last word on the subject was said much later by an amateur poetess who wrote the following verse:

> O Moon, lovely Moon with the beautiful face,
> Careering throughout the bound'ries of space,
> Whenever I see you, I think in my mind—
> Shall I ever, O ever, behold thy behind?

We have not as yet "beheld her behind," but there is no reason to think that it is very different from her face. Meanwhile, Newton himself was doing little scientific work and was deep in his alchemical and mystical studies. Robert Hooke was much more active, and presently he, too, turned his attention to gravitation, producing a book in which he came to much the same conclusions that Newton had. He stated that each heavenly body attracts every other, and that a body moving in a straight line will continue to do so unless interfered with by some outside force.

Hooke also knew that the force between two bodies will become weaker if they are moved farther apart. He even stated that the attractive force must be "inversely as the square of the distance from the centers about which they revolve," and this Inverse Square Law, as it is called, is the most important link in the whole chain of reasoning.

It can be explained without using anything but easy arithmetic. Consider an impossible but convenient case of two planets revolving around the sun, one at a distance of 2 million miles and the other at 5 million miles. 2 squared, or 2 × 2, is 4; 5 squared, or 5 × 5, is 25. Then the force of the sun on the two planets will be as $1/4$ is to $1/25$, and the force on the more distant planet will be only $4/25$ of that on the nearer planet.

If this law is true, it can be shown that each planet will revolve in an orbit that is not a circle, but an ellipse. Newton proved it; Hooke guessed it, but was not a good enough mathematician to follow his argument through to the end. This is no insult to Hooke. He was a man of tremendous ability, but at that time probably only Newton was capable of producing the full answer.

For a few years Hooke and Newton had been on better terms than usual, but shortly after the appearance of Hooke's work the quarrel began again over another mathematical point. Newton made some calculations, but then put them in a drawer and kept them to himself in his usual way. For the moment, nothing more was done.

Then came an important series of discussions among Hooke, Halley and Sir Christopher Wren. In 1684 they talked about gravity in general and the inverse square law in particular and came to the conclusion that the inverse square law must be true. Halley was quite frank; he was not able to prove the law. Nor was Wren. Hooke claimed that he had in fact made all the necessary calculations, and Wren promptly offered to make a present of an expensive book to the first man who could provide a complete proof of the correctness of the inverse square relationship.

Hooke pleaded that he had kept the answer secret and "would conceal it for some time, that others trying and failing might know how to value it when he should make it public." Whether Wren believed him is a matter of opinion; but after some months had passed by without any more information from Hooke, Halley went down to Cambridge to consult Newton.

Halley did not mince matters and asked a straightforward question: "If the inverse square law be true, what will be the path of a planet?" Newton's answer was equally straightforward: "An ellipse." Halley was taken aback, and asked how his friend could be so sure. Newton replied: "Why, I have calculated it." It must have come as a surprise to learn that Newton had had the answer all along without even taking the trouble to let others know.

Actually, Newton had made the calculation so long before that he had lost his notes. Before Halley left Cambridge, however, he had made Newton promise that he would either find the original calculations or do them again, and Newton was as good as his word. The papers failed to come to light, and so he began working afresh. He was held up for some time by a careless mistake in one of his diagrams, but three months after Halley's visit Newton sent him the proof he wanted. Subsequently, Newton presented a short but important paper on the subject to the Royal Society.

Still Halley was not content. He wanted to make

sure that Newton gave his work to the world, and he persuaded him to write a full account in book form. Newton agreed, and during 1685 and 1686 he worked constantly on the book which he called the *Principia Mathematica Philosophiæ Naturalis* (Mathematical Principles of Natural Philosophy), but which is known to everyone simply as the *Principia.*

The whole work took fifteen months to complete, and it has been described as the greatest mental effort ever made by one man. It is also one of the most important scientific works ever produced. It is the *Principia* which has made certain that Newton's name will live for all time. It was, of course, entirely a "one-man" effort; Newton did have an assistant, Humphrey Newton (his namesake, but no relation), but Humphrey merely acted as a clerk. The copy of the manuscript which Isaac Newton finally sent to Halley was in Humphrey's handwriting.

It is quite impossible to describe the *Principia* properly without using advanced mathematics, but it is not hard to show how far Newton had advanced. In the first part of the book, Newton laid down his laws of motion: (1) that the absence of force leads to regular motion in a straight line with regard to any moving body; (2) that change of motion, or "acceleration," is determined by force; and (3) that every action has an equal and opposite reaction. Newton then laid down the general principles of gravitation and proved the inverse square law, which had so baffled Hooke and everyone else.

In the second book of the *Principia* Newton dealt with the motions of fluids and laid the foundations of the science which has now developed into mathematical physics, besides giving a number of brilliant and beautiful experiments. He also showed that old ideas about the planetary movements were hopelessly wrong.

The third book is, however, the most important of all. In it Newton investigated the movements of the bodies in the solar system, treating them not as mere points but as the great globes they really are. He described the behavior of the planets; the motions of the four known moons of Jupiter and the five of Saturn; the causes of the polar flattening of a planet; the precession of the equinoxes; the tides; the movements of comets; methods of finding the real masses of the sun and planets, and much else besides. When we think about all that was contained in the *Principia* we cannot help wondering how even Newton, then a man aged only forty-four, could have discovered so much.

It is known to everyone that the earth is not a perfect globe. It is slightly flattened and is known as an "oblate spheroid"; the diameter measured through the poles is 26 miles shorter than that measured through the equator. This was known even in Newton's day, but Newton was the first to account for it mathematically, and his theoretical value of the flattening was very near what we now know to be the truth. Larger and less dense planets such as Saturn are even more flattened, as can be seen at a glance when they are observed through a telescope. In the case of Saturn, the polar diameter is 7,000 miles shorter than the equatorial. It must of course be remembered that Saturn is a tremendous globe large enough to hold 763 earths, though the material which makes it up is so much less dense that the total mass of Saturn is only 95 times that of the earth.

This polar flattening of our world is responsible for a gradual shift in the direction of the axis. There is an equatorial bulge, and the sun and moon pull upon this bulge, causing the earth to turn very slowly somewhat as a spinning top does before it falls. At the moment the axis points to a part of the sky very near the bright star Polaris, and so the heavens seem to turn around Polaris once a day. As the axis shifts, however, the north pole of the sky will move away from Polaris, and our remote descendants will have a new pole star—the brilliant Vega—while to the Egyptians of several thousand years ago the pole was close to Thuban, a much fainter star in the constellation of the Dragon. This precession of the equinoxes, as it is called, had been discovered by the Greeks 200 years before Christ, but its cause had been hopelessly misunderstood until Newton explained it.

Another section of the *Principia* dealt with the tides,

which Newton showed to be due to the pull of the moon and, to a lesser extent, the sun. The general theory is shown in Fig. 10, which of course is not to scale.

Let us first suppose that the earth is surrounded by a uniform shell of water, as in the diagram. The moon pulls on this water and produces a heap at the point A, while another heap is produced at the far point B. We can ignore the moon's orbital motion for the moment and consider only the earth's 24-hour rotation upon its axis. The earth spins, but the water heap will not spin with it; it will keep at point A, beneath the moon, and the high tides will thus sweep right around the earth once a day.

Things are not actually so simple as this, since the oceans are irregular in depth and distribution, but the diagram does give a perfectly sound explanation of why the tides occur. The sun causes its own tides, but these are far weaker than the lunar ones, on account of the sun's greater distance. When the sun is at S_1 in the diagram, it is pulling in the same direction as the moon, so the tides are strong (spring tides), whereas when the position is with the moon at M and the sun at S_2 the two tide raisers are pulling against each other, and the tides are weaker (neap). Newton proved all this by applying his law of gravitation.

Equally striking was his description of how comets move. A comet is not a solid body like a planet; it is made up of a swarm of small particles enveloped in thin gas and is much less substantial than even a small planet. Consequently, a comet can be seen only when it is fairly close to the earth. Up to Newton's time it had been believed that comets moved in a fashion all their own, but Newton showed that they obey the same rules as all other bodies in the solar system. Fittingly enough, a striking practical proof was given by Halley.

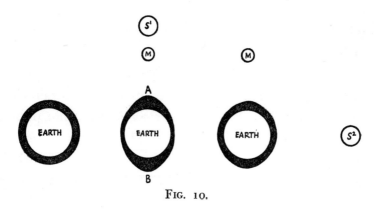

FIG. 10.

Halley had observed a bright comet which appeared in the year 1682. On looking back through the old records, he found that other bright comets had been seen in 1607 and in 1531. The interval between 1531 and 1607 is 76 years, and the interval between 1607 and 1682 is almost the same. Halley therefore used Newton's work to make the bold statement that the three bodies were really one and the same comet, and that it moved around the sun in an elliptical orbit, taking about 76 years to do so.

He then worked out the orbit, taking into account

the disturbing effects of the planets, and forecast that
the comet would be seen again in the year 1758. He
knew that by then he would be dead, but he made the
modest claim that if the comet did indeed return people
would "not refuse to acknowledge that this was first
discovered by an Englishman." On Christmas Day,
1758, a German amateur astronomer named Palitzsch
discovered the comet very close to where Halley had
said it would appear, and it swung around the sun just
as he had predicted. Halley's Comet was last seen at its
return in 1910, and it is due back once more in 1986.

Even now we have not told the full story of how much
the world owes to Halley. The *Principia* was not published without further dispute. Hooke was bitterly
offended at Newton's failure to mention his own work,
as he considered that the proof of the inverse square
law was due largely to him. It is of course true that
Hooke, Halley and Wren had all discussed the law
before they knew of Newton's calculations, but none of
them could prove it—as Halley was the first to admit—
and Newton could have written the *Principia* even if
he had never heard of Hooke's labors. On the other
hand, it would have done Newton no harm to acknowledge Hooke more fully in his preface; he would have
lost nothing by so doing. The truth of the matter was
that the two men were ready to find any excuse for
quarreling. At one stage, Newton was so irritated that
he threatened to keep the vital third book of the *Prin-*

cipia to himself, and it took all Halley's tact to persuade him to allow publication to go on.

There was another source of difficulty. Halley's original idea was that the book should be published by the Royal Society, and at first there was no argument about this. Unfortunately, the Society was short of money. It had just published a tremendous book by Francis Willoughby called *The History of Fishes,* and it seemed that people were no longer particularly interested in fishes, since the book did not sell satisfactorily and caused the Society heavy loss. Halley was not prepared to wait. He probably realized that unless Newton's book appeared promptly, fresh quarrels might prevent its ever being published at all; and he therefore offered to pay for it himself. A resolution passed by the Society states that "Mr. Newton's book be printed in quarto, and that Mr. Halley undertake the business of looking after it and printing it at his own charge, which he engaged to do."

Halley was a younger man than Newton, and on the whole it seems strange that he was allowed to run such a risk, but as things turned out he did not lose by it. The book caused tremendous excitement all over Europe, and by 1691 copies of it were very hard to obtain.

Even then Halley had not heard the last of *The History of Fishes*. Later on he was appointed to a paid position in the Royal Society, and at one period his salary had not been brought up to date; £50 was still owing to him. Instead of giving him the money, the Society awarded him fifty copies of *The History of Fishes,* plus a further twenty copies for back payments. Halley had a strong sense of humor, but whether he was amused or not remains uncertain. Nor is it known what finally became of the seventy books about fishes.

Those two years, 1685 to 1686, were almost as important in Newton's life as were the two plague years that
he spent at Woolsthorpe. He was not only writing the
Principia; he was carrying on with his studies of alchemy
and mysticism, and according to his assistant Humphrey
he used to spend long periods completely lost in thought.
When he woke in the morning he would often forget
to finish dressing and would sit on the edge of his bed
with his mind thousands of miles away among the
planets and stars. At other times he would forget his
lunch or dinner and would leave his meal on the table
uneaten. As Newton had not married and had nobody
to look after him, he was always careless about such
matters; this may have been one cause of his breakdown
some years afterward.

He had the gift of absolute concentration. He would
see the way to tackle a problem, and then he would
work single-mindedly at it until it had been solved,
even if it meant inventing a completely new optical
arrangement or a completely new branch of mathematics in the process.

One last point about the *Principia* may be of interest.
The final permission to print the book was signed by
the then president of the Royal Society, who happened
to be Samuel Pepys. Pepys was not himself a scientist,
but he was one of England's most famous men of litera-
ture, and his diaries have given us the best recorded

picture of life under the last two Stuart kings, Charles II and James II. It was a happy chance that his name is linked with Newton's, even though Newton and his book will be remembered long after the greatness of Pepys has been forgotten.

Chapter 8

FROM SCIENCE TO PARLIAMENT

UP TO NOW we have seen Newton purely as a scientist. His studies of optics, mathematics and gravitation had made him one of the most famous men in England, but he had had little to do with more worldly matters. He had held no public appointments apart from scientific ones, and certainly he had had no connection with politics.

Newton was, in fact, far too honest to become a conventional politician, but at about the time of the publication of the *Principia* he became drawn into a dispute which was partly political and partly to do with the Church. It seemed minor enough at the time, but its results were far-reaching.

Times had changed. Charles II died in 1685, gay and carefree to the last, and in his place reigned his brother James II, the former Duke of York. James and Charles differed in almost every way. Charles may have been selfish and unreliable, but he was neither cruel nor revengeful; provided that he was left to go his own way, he was content for his subjects to think for themselves. James, on the other hand, was a cruel man with none of Charles's good humor. He was far more honest and sincere, but it is significant that whereas Charles reigned for a quarter of a century and ended his days in a stronger position than that in which he had begun, James was driven out by his subjects after only three years.

The main cause of James's downfall was his religion. At that time the Protestants and the Roman Catholics were bitterly opposed to each other, and although England had become a thoroughly Protestant country James Stuart was a Catholic king. (Charles also had probably held Catholic views, but he kept them to himself.)

Had James been content to worship in his own way without interfering with others, all would have been well, but unfortunately for him he was determined to change England back into a Roman Catholic country. Gradually he began to dismiss Protestants from their high positions, replacing them with his own Catholic friends. After a time he forced the University of Oxford to accept a certain John Massey as Dean of Christ Church. Massey had no qualifications to suit him for the post; but he was a Catholic, and in the face of the king's direct order Oxford gave way.

James then turned his attention to Cambridge, and

in February 1687 he demanded that Father Alban Francis, a Benedictine monk, be granted a Master of Arts degree without taking the usual oaths of loyalty to the King and the Church.

At once there was trouble. The Vice-Chancellor, Dr. Pechell, would have been quite ready to do as the king wished if Francis had agreed to take the necessary oaths, but Francis refused. James was furious and summoned Pechell to appear before the High Commission Court at Westminster. Pechell was allowed to take eight other university representatives with him, and one of those chosen was Newton.

The president of the court was the well-known Judge Jeffreys. Jeffreys was probably the most hated man in England, and it is safe to say that he is one of the most unpleasant figures in all history; it was he who had conducted the terrible "Bloody Assizes" following the rebellion led by the Duke of Monmouth, earlier in James's reign. Jeffreys was a cruel, foul-mouthed bully, and when he himself faced danger he showed that he was also a coward.

Pechell was not equipped to stand up to such a man, and Jeffreys soon reduced him to silence. When the other university men tried to speak, Jeffreys ordered them from the court, and it is said that while they were outside Newton encouraged them to do all they could to resist the royal demand. Finally Jeffreys dismissed them with the words: "I will send you home with a text of Scripture: 'Go your way and sin no more, lest a worse thing happen to you.' " Pechell himself was removed from his office as Vice-Chancellor, nor was he allowed to continue as Master of Magdalene College.

However, events were moving quickly. The Cambridge authorities were among the first who tried to defy James, but Father Francis was never in fact given the degree; before many months had passed James too was gone, driven out by the bloodless "Glorious Revolution," and Jeffreys had been thrown into the Tower of London, where he died regretted by nobody.

Newton had taken a leading part in the dispute between Cambridge University and the king, and it was not at all surprising that after James's downfall the "Convention Parliament," which was largely responsible for inviting William of Orange and his wife Mary to share the throne, included what the historian Macaulay called "the majestic forehead and pensive face of Isaac Newton . . . He sat there, in his modest greatness, the unobtrusive but unflinching friend of civil and religious freedom."

Newton sat as Member of Parliament for Cambridge University for a year and a month. It is true that he took very little part in political debates, but he was a keen supporter of the new king and queen and did much to keep Cambridge loyal to them. He belonged to the party now known as the Whigs (the forerunners of the modern Liberals) and was very much against any kind of interference with the religion of others, partly no doubt because his own views were not completely orthodox.

As a matter of fact, Newton did have one more short period in Parliament years later. In the reign of Queen Anne, he was persuaded to seek election once more as representative of the university. He was elected, but seven months later there was a new election; the Whigs had become unpopular, and Newton was defeated by the Tory candidate. As he was by then over sixty years old, he made no further political efforts.

At the time when James was driven out, Newton had reached the height of his powers. He had already gone further than any physicist before him, and probably Halley and his other friends expected even greater work in the future. Unfortunately, matters did not work out in such a way. Newton was coming to the darkest period of his whole life, and there were even rumors that he had gone mad.

He had a great deal to trouble him, and worst of all was the death of his mother, to whom he had always been devoted. He left his science, his parliamentary duties and everything else in order to go home and nurse her; but it was of no use, and Newton was bitterly grieved.

There is another story of this period which should be repeated. It is as follows: "Newton kept a small dog named Diamond, of which he was very fond. When Newton had gone to bed one night, Diamond upset a candle, causing a fire in the laboratory and burning some priceless papers. Newton could say only: 'O Diamond! Diamond! thou little knowest the mischief done!' and was so upset that he suffered a collapse of the kind we should now call a nervous breakdown. Even when he recovered, months later, he was never the brilliant scientist that he had been before."

There is not a word of truth in the whole tale. There had indeed been a small fire in Newton's laboratory, but it had happened years earlier, before the *Principia* had even been begun; Newton never had a dog—his assistant Humphrey says plainly that "he kept neither dog nor cat"—and no papers of any value were lost. The whole story of Diamond is as false as the older, pleasanter fable of King Canute and the waves.

On the other hand it is correct to say that Newton did have a nervous breakdown. He was not "mad" in any sense of the word, but he was thoroughly upset, and he sent strange letters to some of his friends accusing them of turning against him.

The strain of writing the *Principia* must have been tremendous. There was also the added strain of the disputes with James II, and Newton's grief at the death of his mother. Moreover, he had done his best to find some government appointment which would give him a rest from pure science, and he had not been successful. All these things combined to cause his breakdown, and on the whole it is surprising not that such a breakdown came, but that it did not come long before 1692.

Newton was fortunate in his friends, none of whom took any real notice of his curious behavior. Naturally enough, the foreign scientists who had corresponded with Newton were distressed to hear of his illness, particularly as some of them believed it to be far worse than was really the case. Christiaan Huygens, with whom Newton had often disagreed, seems actually to have believed that he had gone insane, as we learn from some of the letters written by him to Leibnitz.

Gradually Newton recovered. The illness had left its mark on him, and it may be true to say that he never recaptured the old wish to "find out," but by 1694 he was to all intents and purposes himself once more. His brain remained as keen and brilliant as ever, and although his greatest triumphs lay in the past his scientific career was by no means at an end.

Chapter 9

THE MASTER OF THE MINT

IT MAY sound strange that a man like Newton, the most brilliant scientist of his time, should want to take a perfectly ordinary government appointment. Yet this is just what Newton did. There were periods when he seemed to become tired of science, and after his illness he never regained his enthusiasm for optics or mathematics, even though his ability was as great as ever.

Even before the downfall of James II, Newton seems to have wanted an official position, but for some time he was disappointed. After his thirteen months in Parliament, his illness forced him to give up most of his normal activities for a while, and he was fortunate that his friends were not offended by the strange letters which he wrote to them.

One man whom Newton accused of being "false to him" was Charles Montague, one of his closest friends. He was eighteen years Newton's junior, and the two had first met while Montague was an undergraduate at Cambridge. The younger man was clever, ambitious and witty, and as he was also a member of a noble family he soon made his way in politics. He entered Parliament in 1689, at the same time as Newton, but whereas Newton's political career virtually ended in the following year, Montague's carried him on to the heights. He became Chancellor of the Exchequer in 1694 and was afterward given the title of Lord Halifax. Finally he was able to offer the post which Newton so much wanted. Two years later, he wrote Newton a letter beginning "I am very glad that at last I can give you a good proof of my friendship, and the esteem the King has of your merits," and offering him the Wardenship of the Royal Mint.

The Mint is the place where the country's coins are made, and a few words about coinage in general will help to make clear the kind of work that Newton had to do. Money has been used since very early times; the original method of exchange or barter was obviously limited, and some sort of coin was much more satisfactory. Metal was used to make coins because it is light to carry and is not easily damaged. Silver and brass were popular, and at first they were simply exchanged by weight for other materials of all kinds.

A vague system of this sort was bound to lead to trouble, and even before the Norman Conquest attempts were made to give England a standard coinage. The first man to succeed was Alfred's grandson, King Athelstan. Athelstan was one of the best rulers England ever had, and between the years 925 and 941 he governed his country with a firm but kindly hand; he was a fearless soldier who proved more than a match for all his enemies, and, like Alfred, he was deeply interested in learning and in the welfare of his subjects. He drew up laws for the organization of the mints, and made fixed rules that the money-makers had to follow.

Centuries later, when Edward II was king, new laws were made, and these form the basis of the laws in force today in England. Each mint had a Master, a Warden and other officers. Gradually, too, the mints outside London were closed down. That in Winchester remained for some time, but by the end of the seventeenth century only the London Mint remained.

When Montague became Chancellor, he found the country's coinage in a very bad way. The standard coins were of gold and silver, but much of the money in circulation was made up of damaged coins which had been reduced in value by having pieces chopped off them. Since the actual value of a coin depended on the amount of metal in it, an average "shilling" was actually worth no more than sixpence. The only thing to do was to call in all the old coins and replace them with new ones of proper weight and size and with "milled" edges so that they could not be chopped up.

Clearly, a dishonest Mint official would have tremendous opportunities to make himself rich, and when the recoinage scheme was in progress it was most important to have honest men in charge. Montague chose Newton, and in this he was wise. Newton may have been moody, shy and uncertain-tempered, but dishonesty was not in his nature, and he soon showed that he was as capable in official matters as he had been in the field of science.

Oddly enough, he was not in favor of new ideas. In science he was forever developing fresh methods, but as Warden of the Mint he preferred to keep to the tested schemes laid down by those before him. He was not concerned only with the actual coinage. He had to keep a close watch for counterfeiters, makers of illegal coins, and he actually managed to catch the ringleader; he was made a justice of the peace, and he interviewed lawyers and criminals himself instead of leaving such matters to his assistants. In short, Newton became a capable and worthy government servant.

This does not mean that he was responsible for the whole recoinage scheme. He did not become Warden until the first difficulties were over, and the actual plan was not his; but he certainly carried it through very well—Montague is said to have remarked that he could not have managed properly without Newton's help— and it was not surprising when, in 1699, he was appointed Master of the Mint. This solved all his own money troubles. His salary was something like £2,000 a year, which meant that he had become a rich man.

He remained Master until his death, though after the
end of the recoinage scheme there was much less work
to do and often in his later years he did not have to go
to the Mint at all.

His government duties meant, of course, that he had
to live in London. He therefore set up house in Jermyn
Street, where he was joined by his clever and beautiful
niece Catherine Barton, a close friend of Montague's.
During his Wardenship he kept his positions at Cambridge, but when he became Master of the Mint he
appointed the Rev. William Whiston as his deputy
"with the full profits of the place." In 1701 Newton
resigned his Lucasian Chair, and this meant also his
surrender of the fellowship of Trinity, so that his official
link with Cambridge University was broken. Whiston,
incidentally, was expelled from the university in 1710
for his unpopular religious views. His ideas were not
unlike Newton's own; but while Newton kept silent,
Whiston did not—and paid the penalty, though expul-
sion from Cambridge was a very mild punishment compared with those inflicted on Bruno and Galileo in the
previous century. Newton said nothing in Whiston's
defense, and it has been argued that under the circum-
stances he ought to have done so.

It is worth while telling another story, this time a
true one, to show that Newton still kept his old scientific
brilliance even after he became busy at the Mint. In
1696 the famous Swiss mathematician Jean Bernouilli

set his fellow mathematicians a very difficult problem and challenged them to solve it within six months, promising that if nobody could do so he would publish his own answer. No solution was forthcoming, but, in a letter to Bernouilli, Leibnitz said that he had "cut the knot" of the problem and asked to be allowed a little longer to work it out fully.

Newton first saw the problem on January 29, 1697, and solved it the same evening. Next day he sent his answer to Montague, who was then president of the Royal Society, and it was passed on to Bernouilli. Two other correct answers were received later, one from Leibnitz and the other from the Marquis de l'Hôpital, but Newton's was the best, and Bernouilli guessed the author of it at once, even though the papers were sent to him without his being told who was responsible. Some years later, Leibnitz himself set a challenge which Newton received in the afternoon and solved before going to bed. So much for the tale that his scientific genius vanished forever after his breakdown in 1692!

Newton was now famous not only for his science, but for his work in the service of the nation. He had still more than a quarter of a century to live, and probably he was as content as his restless nature allowed him to be.

Chapter 10

"SIR ISAAC NEWTON"

ALTHOUGH Newton had taken up an important position in the Mint and spent more time on what he called "the King's business" than on mathematical and optical problems, he was still regarded as being England's leading man of science. His illness was a thing of the past, and he was himself again, so even if he did not wish to turn back wholly to science he could still solve the most difficult problems whenever called upon to do so.

His fame was not confined to Britain. His first great honor, indeed, came from France. In 1699 the famous Paris Academy of Sciences was reorganized, and eight Foreign Associates were named. Among them were Leibnitz of Germany, the great mathematician; Bernouilli of Switzerland, who had set the famous "challenge"; Römer of Denmark, who had first calculated the velocity of light; and Isaac Newton of England.

Unfortunately Newton had never lost his dislike of criticism, and even during his busiest period at the Mint he fell out with the Astronomer Royal, John Flamsteed. It is not easy to see who was principally to blame. Flamsteed had all Newton's faults together with others of his own, but there was some excuse for him, since he was a sick man and was in constant difficulty over money. (His salary as Astronomer Royal was so small that he had to go on acting as vicar of a parish in order to make ends meet.)

The cause of the original dispute was simple enough. Newton had begun working upon the problems set by the motions of the moon, and he naturally needed to know the exact way in which the moon was moving across the sky. The only person able to give him this information was Flamsteed, who was busy working away at Greenwich Observatory. At first Flamsteed was ready to help, and there are no signs of any quarrel before Newton's illness. Afterward, however, Newton wanted more information than Flamsteed was ready to provide. It will be remembered that Flamsteed was a man who disliked publishing anything until it had been checked and rechecked again to his complete satisfaction.

Newton's reputation was even greater than Flamsteed's, and he tried to force observations from the Astronomer Royal, demanding them as though he had every right to them. Dislike took the place of the former friendly relations between the two, and finally a bitter quarrel broke out which was never healed. Later on, when there was trouble about the delay in publishing Flamsteed's star catalogue, Halley was drawn into the dispute, and it must be admitted that the affair reflects no credit upon any of those who took part in it.

Robert Hooke died in 1703. It would be unjust and ungenerous to say that this was a relief to Newton, but it is true that after the death of the sour, luckless genius, Newton felt more free to publish his past work. He had deliberately kept back many of his studies about light because he knew that Hooke would at once attack them, and though Newton could have given a full answer he did not like the idea of yet another quarrel.

However we look at the matter, it is a tragedy that Newton and Hooke could not manage to overcome their dislike for each other. Each had a brain of unusual brilliance; could they have worked together, science would have been much the richer. It is generally stated that Hooke was wholly to blame, but this is not quite fair. Newton was not an easy person, and the greatest geniuses are only human.

Safe from Hooke's tongue, Newton began to prepare his papers for the press. In 1704 he produced his book *Opticks*, which is second in importance only to the *Principia* itself. It must be remembered, however, that most of the work had been done before his illness, and certainly before he went to the Mint, so that the actual writing of the book did not need a mental effort as great as that involved in compiling the *Principia*. One interesting point about *Opticks* is that it was written in English. Most scientific works of the period were in Latin, and this was the language of the *Principia*, though some men (notably Hooke) always wrote in their own tongue.

By the time *Opticks* appeared, Newton had been given yet another honor, that of the presidency of the Royal Society. Nowadays a president must be a leading man of science, but during the half-century following the formation of the Society in 1660 this was not always the case; Pepys, who was president when the *Principia* was written, was certainly no scientist, nor for that matter was Charles Montague. But Newton's claims to the position were so obvious that they could not be passed over, and he succeeded to the presidency in 1703 upon the retirement of Lord Somers. He remained as such until his death, and he presided over his last meeting only twenty days before he died.

Meanwhile there had been a change of sovereigns in England. William of Orange was dead, and in his place reigned Queen Anne, the younger daughter of James II. Anne's husband was Prince George of Denmark, who has left little mark on English history, but who was deeply interested in science and the arts. Prince George was always very friendly toward Newton, for whom he had a great respect, and it was on Newton's recommendation that he offered to pay for the printing of the observations made by Flamsteed at Greenwich. He was also elected a Fellow of the Royal Society.

Queen Anne thought equally highly of Newton, and before long she showed her respect publicly. In April 1705 she, Prince George and the court were staying at Newmarket, which is not far from Cambridge, and she paid a visit to the university as a guest of the Master of Trinity College. While there, the queen presented honorary degrees to various members of the college and, finally, conferred an Order of Knighthood upon Cambridge's most famous man, Isaac Newton.

It is important to remember that the knighthood was given not for services to the government (his work at the Mint), but for services to science. His government work was not of vital importance, and had Newton done nothing but look after the recoinage scheme he would not be remembered today. (Even Lord Halifax, Chancellor of the Exchequer and a leading politician of the time, would have been forgotten long ago but for his connection with Newton.) But Newton's scientific labors were in a class of their own, and it is pleasant to think that his greatness was recognized by his queen.

Newton was the first scientist to be honored in such a way. Over a century passed before another public award was given for such work, when Humphry Davy, inventor of the safety lamp, was created a baronet.

Sir Isaac was now a man of over sixty, and since the busiest period of the recoinage scheme was over he could afford to spend more time on scientific work. The days when he spent weeks or months in constant study were past, but it seems that he became less restless as he grew older, and when it was suggested to him that the time had come for a new edition of the *Principia* he was ready to agree. He did not wish to see to it on his own, but he made a large number of written notes in the margin of a copy of the first edition, and the preparation of the new version was left to a brilliant young Fellow of Trinity College named Roger Cotes.

Newton was never slow to see ability in others, and he had a very high opinion of Cotes, so there were no disputes between the two. All went smoothly. Work actually began in 1709, and four years later the new edition was published. Newton went personally to Queen Anne in order to give her a copy of it.

It was a tragedy for science that Cotes did not live to fulfill the promise of his youth. He died before he was thirty-five, and Newton himself was moved to say, "If Mr. Cotes had lived, we might have known something!" which was high praise indeed.

Chapter 11

THE LAST YEARS

Sir Isaac Newton had become one of the best-known men in the realm. He was president of the Royal Society and was acknowledged to be England's leading scientist; his name was a byword all over Europe, and no foreign visitor of importance was content to visit London without meeting him; he was respected even by nonscientists for his honest and effective handling of the Mint recoinage, and he was a popular figure at court. This remained the case even after the death of Queen Anne; the Princess of Wales (afterward Queen Caroline, wife of George II) had the greatest regard for him and is said to have "lost no opportunity of talking with him."

It would be pleasant to record that Newton's later years were free of the quarrels and arguments which had followed him all through his public life, but unhappily this was not the case. Hooke was dead, but

Newton was still to continue his dispute with Flamsteed and to come into bitter conflict with Leibnitz.

The Flamsteed trouble began first. Newton had already irritated the Astronomer Royal by his demand for observations of the moon, but evidently this breach had healed to some extent, for in April 1704 we find the two men dining together at Greenwich, apparently on friendly terms. Newton had had a special reason for his visit; he wanted to learn how far Flamsteed had progressed with his star catalogue, since other astronomers were beginning to grow impatient with the delay in publishing it.

Flamsteed said that he was almost ready for printing arrangements to be made, and in the following November he described his observations and plans in a letter to the Royal Society. It was then that Prince George of Denmark made his generous offer to pay for the catalogue, and the Society formed a special committee to examine Flamsteed's manuscripts and report on them. The committee—made up of five men, including Newton and Wren—recommended that all the observations should be published.

Still Flamsteed was not quite ready, and he handed the committee a copy of his observations and also an incomplete manuscript of his star catalogue. He made it clear that the catalogue was not be printed as it stood, but was to wait until it had been completed and checked; the observations, however, could go forward, and printing duly began.

For a number of reasons, including the death of Prince George in 1708, the printing was slow. Still Flamsteed did not produce the final version of his star catalogue, for which all his fellow astronomers were waiting. It has been claimed that because Flamsteed was Astronomer Royal, and as such a servant of his country, he should have produced the catalogue as a matter of duty, but this view is not completely fair to Flamsteed. It is true that he held a paid position, but his salary was very small —as we have seen, he had to make ends meet by acting as vicar of a parish—and when he had been installed in Greenwich Observatory, by order of Charles II, he had not even been given any instruments, which he had had to provide himself. (His widow reclaimed them when he died, so the second Astronomer Royal, Halley, had to begin all over again.)

Fresh causes of dispute arose. In 1710 Queen Anne appointed a "Board of Visitors" to inspect Greenwich Observatory each year and to force the Astronomer Royal to give them the results of his work. Newton headed the board, and Flamsteed was violently offended; he resented what he thought to be interference with his personal business, and he had a good deal of right on his side, though his own stubbornness had caused the trouble in the first place. The patched-up friendship between Flamsteed and Newton was definitely broken.

Matters came to a head in 1711, with the publication of Flamsteed's observations. They took the form of one large book, which contained not only the observations which Flamsteed had passed for publication, but also the star catalogue, which he had not. It is clear that the commitee had become tired of waiting for the Astronomer Royal to finish the catalogue himself and had asked Halley to make the best of things. Halley had therefore supplied whole pages of material on his own, and he had added a preface which could not be anything but harmful to Flamsteed's reputation.

Flamsteed's anger can well be pictured. He held Newton chiefly responsible, since as president of the Royal Society it was he who had (so it was said) promised that that catalogue should not be issued in its unfinished form; but Flamsteed hated Halley even more fiercely and lost no chance of attacking him.

All that Flamsteed could do was revise the catalogue as far as he could and then publish it at his own expense. He wanted to do the same with the observations, but Newton held some of the manuscripts and Flamsteed was unable to get them back. When a new Lord Chamberlain was appointed, in 1715, a large number of copies of the original publication fell into Flamsteed's hands, and he immediately burned all the catalogues "that none might remain to show the ingratitude of two of his countrymen"—by whom he meant, of course, Newton and Halley. Actually he did not live to finish the revision, but the work was completed by two of his assistants, Crosthwait and Sharp, who published the final result in 1725.

The three-cornered battle between Newton, Flamsteed and Halley does no credit to any of them. Newton showed a good deal of bad temper, Flamsteed's behavior was childish and vicious, and even Halley cannot escape criticism completely, since his preface to the original catalogue could have been written in more tactful terms.

Equally unfortunate was the quarrel with Leibnitz, which had far-reaching results. This was not merely a personal argument between two or three men; all the leading mathematicians of Europe were drawn in, as well as the Royal Society itself, and even King George I took an interest, though it is doubtful whether he understood much of what it was all about.

The point at issue was whether Newton or Leibnitz had been the first to invent that branch of mathematics known nowadays as calculus, but which Newton called the "method of fluxions." There can be little doubt that each made the discovery more or less independently, and nowadays we can only wonder why the matter caused as much bitterness as it did.

There is no point in trying to describe calculus in detail, but it may be said to be that branch of mathematics which deals with changing quantities and with the rate of change of a given quantity. Newton had had to develop it, as otherwise he would have been unable to finish off some of his calculations; in fact, he had some correspondence with Leibnitz about his "method of fluxions" as early as 1676, before he had become world-famous. Leibnitz, on the other hand, was interested in figures for their own sake and did not share Newton's view that mathematics is merely a tool to be used in other investigations.

Whether Leibnitz gained his original ideas from Newton is not clear, but in three papers published between 1684 and 1686 he gave an account of the calculus, developed in a form which made it much more easy to use than Newton's. It was at once taken up by other scientists, and became widely used all over Europe for the solving of difficult and important problems.

Finally Newton did publish his own "method of fluxions," which was essentially the same as Leibnitz' calculus. Leibnitz apparently thought that he had been copied, and he wrote an unsigned review of Newton's *Opticks* in which he said plainly that Newton was trying to claim a discovery which had in fact been made by Leibnitz.

English mathematicians were violently angry. In 1708 John Keill, of Oxford, wrote a paper in which he said that it was Leibnitz who had taken the idea from some correspondence between Newton and Oldenburg which he had had the opportunity to read. Leibnitz was equally furious. He protested to the Royal Society and asked them to force Keill to apologize and withdraw his paper. Keill refused.

Feelings ran so high that the Royal Society had to take action, and it appointed a committee to examine the whole matter. A report was printed in 1712 in which Newton's claim was supported, but since Newton himself was president of the Royal Society, while Halley had served on the committee, Leibnitz was even angrier than before. He began to attack Newton on other grounds also, and it was then that he challenged Newton to solve a problem which could not be worked out except by a man who had complete mastery of the calculus—or the "method of fluxions," which it was called. As we know, Newton received the problem one afternoon and had the answer before going to bed.

The quarrel would certainly have continued for years more, but Leibnitz died in 1716, and tempers gradually cooled. However, the whole business had unhappy results. Leibnitz' methods were far easier to use, but for a long time British mathematicians refused to use them; they preferred to follow Newton's clumsier "fluxions," and it was not for another hundred years that calculus as Leibnitz had perfected it became widely used in England.

Why was Newton drawn into so many quarrels with his scientific companions? He had been bitterly attacked first by Hooke, then by Flamsteed and lastly by Leibnitz, all of whom nevertheless respected his unique gifts. Jealousy of Newton may have been partly responsible, at least in the case of Hooke, but a little tact on both sides would have done much to smooth matters over. The final verdict must be that while Newton was much more sinned against than sinning, he was not entirely free from blame.

He was now an old man, and he lived long enough to learn of the deaths of many of his friends and opponents—Barrow, Huygens, Hooke, Lord Halifax, Cotes, Leibnitz, Flamsteed, Wren and many others. Of those with whom he had been closely associated, only Halley outlived him. Yet Newton's mind was as strong and vigorous as ever. He spent much time studying ancient history, and his last work, *The Chronology of Ancient Kingdoms,* was not actually published until after his death. He still spent a certain amount of time at the Mint and continued to preside at meetings of the Royal Society (though it is on record that he once fell asleep in the middle of listening to a paper). He even helped to prepare a third edition of his greatest work, the *Principia,* which was carried through by a brilliant young mathematician named Henry Pemberton and was published in 1726.

Halley succeeded Flamsteed as Astronomer Royal, and the honor done to his friend must have given Newton much pleasure. It should be added that Newton acted most generously to Pemberton and to other young scientists who he thought showed real promise. There was, for instance, the case of Colin Maclaurin. Maclaurin, a twenty-six-year-old Scot, applied for an important post in Edinburgh; Newton thought highly of him and not only supported his claim but even offered to add twenty pounds per year to his salary in order to make it possible for him to go there. Maclaurin obtained the position and later became one of the best mathematicians in Scottish history.

The third edition of the *Principia* appeared when Newton was eighty-four, and it marked the end of his scientific work. He had carried his years extremely well; his sight, his hearing and his brain remained keen, and he never lost his hair or his teeth. But at last he was beginning to fail, and he had to spend much of his time at his Kensington home, thinking and reading.

On February 28, 1727, he attended his last meeting of the Royal Society; when he returned home six days later it became clear that he was seriously ill. He was tended by two of the best doctors in the country, and on March 15 he seemed a little better, but the end was near. He drifted into unconsciousness at six o'clock in the evening of March 18 and died painlessly in his sleep at half-past one in the morning of March 20.

Newton had become almost a legendary figure; it was hard for his companions to believe that he had left them, and every possible honor was given him. His body lay in state and then was buried in Westminster Abbey. The Abbey is the tomb of England's kings, and it was fitting that Newton's earthly remains should be placed at rest in such a national shrine.

No king is more worthy to lie there.

Chapter 12

OUR DEBT TO NEWTON

SIR ISAAC NEWTON died two and a quarter centuries ago, but since then his name has become even more famous than it was during his lifetime. No one person before or since has ever made a greater contribution to man's understanding of the universe, and much of today's scientific thought is based on laws that he formulated.

We have already mentioned the man-made satellites, which spin in their orbits hundreds of miles above the earth in accordance with Newton's law of universal gravitation. This was not his only contribution to our "miniature moons," however. These marvels of our age must be launched by rocket power, because above a height of a few miles the air is so thin that none of our ordinary aircraft will work; the rocket, however, operates on Newton's old principle that "every action has an equal and positive reaction," and it functions best in outer space where there is no air at all. In any rocket, the power is supplied by a rush of gas out of the exhaust. As the gas comes out, it "kicks" the body of the rocket in the opposite direction; and as long as the gas stream continues, the rocket will keep moving. Fourth of July skyrockets operate on this Principle of Reaction, and so will space ships of the future.

In optics, much of Newton's pioneer work still holds good. He was wrong in his picture of the nature of light, but his ideas as to its behavior were perfectly sound. He was the real founder of "spectroscopy," which has now become one of the most powerful tools of astronomical research.

We remember how Newton first split up white light by passing it through a glass prism and producing a band made up of all the colors of the rainbow. Almost a hundred years after Newton's death, a young German optician named Franhofer developed the prism arrangement by introducing a telescope and a slit as well and found that the bright band was crossed by a large number of curious dark lines. (Strictly speaking, these lines had been seen earlier by Dr. Wollaston of Cambridge, in 1802; but since Wollaston thought they merely marked the boundaries between different colors, the real honor must go to Fraunhofer.)

The dark or "absorption" lines, as they are called, have made it possible for astronomers to investigate the nature of the sun, while the stars—which are themselves suns—show absorption lines of the same type. Newton might easily have discovered the lines himself. He failed to do so, and yet his original experiments with the prism opened the way for the great advances that were to follow.

Newton was mistaken when he said that it would never be possible to make a large refracting telescope free from the false color difficulty, but this error had fortunate results. It led him to make the first reflector, and nowadays reflectors are more important astronomically than refractors. There are several reasons for this. A large mirror is far easier to make than a large lens, and it is also easier to mount. In a refractor the light has to pass through the object glass, and the glass can be supported only around its edge. If the lens is large and heavy, it may start to bend under its own weight, and the slightest distortion will make it useless. Mirrors, on the other hand, can be supported by their undersides, since only the upper surface of a polished mirror is used to reflect the rays of light.

Even when it was shown that good refractors can be made, the reflecting type of telescope kept its lead in astronomy as a whole. Giant instruments came into being. Sir William Herschel built a reflector with a 48-inch mirror; Lord Rosse surpassed this with a 72-inch; then, in our own century, came the two giants of California—the Mount Wilson 100-inch and the Palomar 200-inch, while the Lick Observatory 120-inch is almost completed and the Greenwich 98-inch is in the process of construction. These tremendous instruments have complex optical systems, but most reflecting telescopes in use today follow Newton's original arrangement.

As a matter of fact, Newton can also be credited with the invention of another instrument, the sextant. In 1700 he described his invention in a letter to Halley, but (as usual) he did not publish it, and even Halley apparently failed to see its value. The letter was forgotten, and the sextant was reinvented by John Hadley in 1730. It is interesting to guess how many other ideas of Newton's were lost simply because he failed to make them public.

Newton's laws of motion, and his theory of universal gravitation, have of course provided the foundations upon which all later mathematical astronomy has been built. One famous example is worth repeating, partly because it shows the soundness of his principles and partly because it, too, led to an unhappy dispute.

In 1781, the Hanoverian astronomer William (afterward Sir William) Herschel discovered a new planet, which was christened Uranus. It proved to revolve around the sun at a distance much greater than that of Saturn, which had formerly been regarded as the outermost planet, and before long its orbit had been worked out according to Newton's principles.

Then, for some unknown reason, Uranus started to

stray. Its calculated orbit turned out to be wrong, and
an amateur mathematician named Hussey suggested
that this might be due to the pull of a more distant
planet. The problem was taken up independently by
two mathematicians, John Couch Adams of Cambridge
and Urbain Le Verrier of France. What they had to do
was to find the position of the undiscovered body which
was pulling on Uranus; it was a fascinating "detective
problem" in which the hidden culprit was not a crim-
inal, but a planet. Presently they produced almost the
same answer and found out just where the new world
should be.

Adams sent his results to the then Astronomer Royal,
Sir George Airy, but Airy had little faith in them and
took no action for some time. Le Verrier's answer went
to Professor Galle, at Berlin, and Galle at once began
searching in the position indicated. As soon as Airy
heard what was happening, he sent Adams' papers to
Cambridge Observatory, and there too a search started.

Galle was the victor in the race. Close to Le Verrier's
position he discovered a dim point that soon proved
to be the wanted planet, while the Cambridge observers
did not identify it until later. The quarrel between
Newton and Leibnitz was repeated. Just as Newton had
been the first to invent calculus, so Adams had been the
first to work out the position of the new planet; just as
Leibnitz had been first to publish his results, so Le Verrier's calculations had led to the actual discovery. How-

ever, neither Adams nor Le Verrier took much personal part in the dispute, and honor is now satisfied by the recognition of the two mathematicians as joint dis-coverers of the planet we call Neptune.

The discovery could never have been made without Newton's work, and there are many other examples— one of which, the tracking-down of another unknown planet (now named Pluto), will be remembered by many men now living, as Pluto was found as recently as 1930.

Would these great advances have been made even if Newton had never lived? We must suppose that they would; but probably not all at once, and not in so fin-ished a form, so the progress of science would have been far slower than was actually the case.

Even Newton's alchemical studies have proved of some value. It is true that his search for gold and for the mythical "philosopher's stone" was bound to fail, but he did make a number of chemical advances during his search, and it is even probable that he had a very good idea of the atomic structure of matter—even though he did not say so directly, and it was not his manuscripts which led to the later discovery of atomic structure.

Yet we must think not only of Newton's services to science; we must remember the character of the man himself. He had his faults, as everyone has, and he was not always even-tempered, while his dislike of criticism and argument was one of the reasons why he was drawn into quarrels with men such as Hooke and Leibnitz. But his failings were minor and were far outweighed by his virtues. He was clear-headed, loyal, kindly and generous; he hated cruelty in any form, and he was quick to see good in others and to give help whenever it lay in his power.

So long as humanity lasts, Newton will never be forgotten.

Appendix

SOME IMPORTANT DATES
IN NEWTON'S LIFE

1642   Newton born at Woolsthorpe.

1645   Mrs. Newton remarries, and Isaac is put in his grandmother's charge.

1654   Sent to the King's School, Grantham.

1656   His mother returns to Woolsthorpe.

1658   Withdrawn from King's School, but afterward sent
back.

1661   Enters Trinity College, Cambridge.

1664   Scholarship at Trinity College.

1665   Takes the degree of Bachelor of Arts.

1665–6 Cambridge closed for some time on account of the
plague. Newton stays at Woolsthorpe and lays the
foundations of much of his greatest work.

1667   Elected a Fellow of Trinity College.

1668   Takes the degree of Master of Arts. The first reflecting telescope was probably made by Newton during
this year.

1669   Barrow resigns the Lucasian Chair, and Newton succeeds him.

1671   Dr. Ward proposes him for the Royal Society.

1672   Elected to the Royal Society, presents his first papers on optics, and describes the reflecting telescope. First disputes with Hooke, Huygens and others.

1679   Fresh disputes with Hooke over mathematical matters.

1684   Halley approaches him about the "Inverse Square Law," following discussions with Hooke and Wren.

1685–6 Writes the *Principia*.

1687   Publication of the last volume of the *Principia*. Newton takes a leading part in the dispute between Cambridge University and King James II.

1689–90 Sits as Member of Parliament for Cambridge University.

1692–3 His breakdown.

1696   Appointed Warden of the Mint.

1697   Gives a quick solution of the problem set by Bernouilli.

1699   Made Master of the Mint, and created a Foreign Associate of the French Academy of Sciences.

1701   Resigns his Lucasian Chair in favor of Whiston, and surrenders his Fellowship of Trinity College.

1703   Death of Robert Hooke.
        Newton elected president of the Royal Society.

1704   Publication of the *Opticks*.

1705   Knighted by Queen Anne.

1709   Preparations made for the second edition of the
        Principia, supervised by Cotes.

1713   Second edition of the *Principia* published, and New-
        ton presents a copy to Queen Anne.

1715   Death of Lord Halifax.

1716   Newton gives a quick solution of the problem set by
        Leibnitz. Death of Leibnitz, ending the prolonged
        quarrel about calculus.

1717   Second edition of *Opticks.*

1722   Preparations for the third edition of the *Principia,*
        supervised by Henry Pemberton.

1726   Publication of the third edition of the *Principia.*

1727   Dies at Kensington, and is buried in Westminster
        Abbey.